RAF FIGHTERS
VS
Ju 87 STUKA
In the West 1940–41

ANDY SAUNDERS

OSPREY PUBLISHING
Bloomsbury Publishing Plc
Kemp House, Chawley Park, Cumnor Hill, Oxford, OX2 9PH, UK
29 Earlsfort Terrace, Dublin 2, Ireland
1385 Broadway, 5th Floor, New York, NY 10018, USA
E-mail: info@ospreypublishing.com
www.ospreypublishing.com

OSPREY is a trademark of Osprey Publishing Ltd

First published in Great Britain in 2024

A catalogue record for this book is available from the British Library.

ISBN: PB: 9781472862570; eBook 9781472862587; ePDF 9781472862556;
XML 9781472862563

24 25 26 27 28 10 9 8 7 6 5 4 3 2 1

Edited by Tony Holmes
Cover artwork and battlescene by Gareth Hector
Three-views, side-views, cockpit views, Engaging the Enemy artwork and
armament views by Jim Laurier
Map and tactical diagram by www.bounford.com
Index by Zoe Ross
Typeset by PDQ Digital Media Solutions, Bungay, UK
Printed by Repro India Ltd.

Osprey Publishing supports the Woodland Trust, the UK's leading woodland
conservation charity.

To find out more about our authors and books visit
www.ospreypublishing.com. Here you will find extracts, author interviews,
details of forthcoming events and the option to sign up for our newsletter.

Spitfire IB cover artwork

On 5 February 1941, four Spitfires of No. 92 Sqn attacked four Ju 87Bs of
2./StG 1 that had been targeting shipping in the Thames Estuary. The four
Spitfires were flown by Plt Offs R. H. Fokes and C. H. Saunders and Sgts
H. Bowen-Morris and C. A. Ream, all four pilots sharing in the destruction
of one of the Stukas. The enemy aircraft was Wk-Nr 5225 J9+BK, which
exploded when it hit the ground near RAF Manston, in Kent, from where
No. 92 Sqn was operating. One of the RAF fighters (as depicted on the cover)
was cannon-armed Spitfire IB R6923 QJ-S. Each of the four pilots was
granted a quarter share in the destruction of the Stuka, it being the last
aircraft of its type brought down on land in the British Isles. (Artwork by
Gareth Hector)

Ju 87B cover artwork

On 16 August 1940, Hauptmann Helmut Mahlke of III./StG 1 led eight
Ju 87 Stukas in an attack on the Chain Home radar station at Ventnor, on the
Isle of Wight. Pursued by Hurricanes, none of Mahlke's aircraft were hit and
all of them returned safely home. Uniquely, Mahlke, as *Gruppenkommandeur,*
had both gear legs of his Ju 87 painted overall yellow to enable the pilots
under his command to easily spot him in the air. Similarly, his *Staffelkapitäne*
had one gear leg of their aircraft painted yellow to aid air-to-air identification.
Mahlke also hoped that the yellow-painted legs would draw the attention of
attacking fighters to him, thus giving his less experienced pilots a better chance
of being left unmolested. (Artwork by Gareth Hector)

Previous page

A 250kg bomb awaits loading onto a Ju 87B of IV.(Stuka)/LG 1 in France in
1940. Of note is the collar with its lugs for locating the weapon onto the
bomb trapeze beneath the Stuka's centreline. (Author's Collection)

Contents

INTRODUCTION

Although the Junkers Ju 87 had seen limited action during the Spanish Civil War, and again in the skies over Poland following the German invasion in September 1939, any serious or specific thought as to how the squadrons of RAF Fighter Command might counter the type in battle had not been given. Generally, the established RAF tactics for dealing with bomber aircraft prior to the outbreak of war had largely been predicated on the notion of the interception of large formations of conventional bomber types.

In the context of these tactics, the received wisdom was that set-piece standard attack scenarios (Fighter Attacks Nos. 1, 2 and 3) would be adopted against bomber

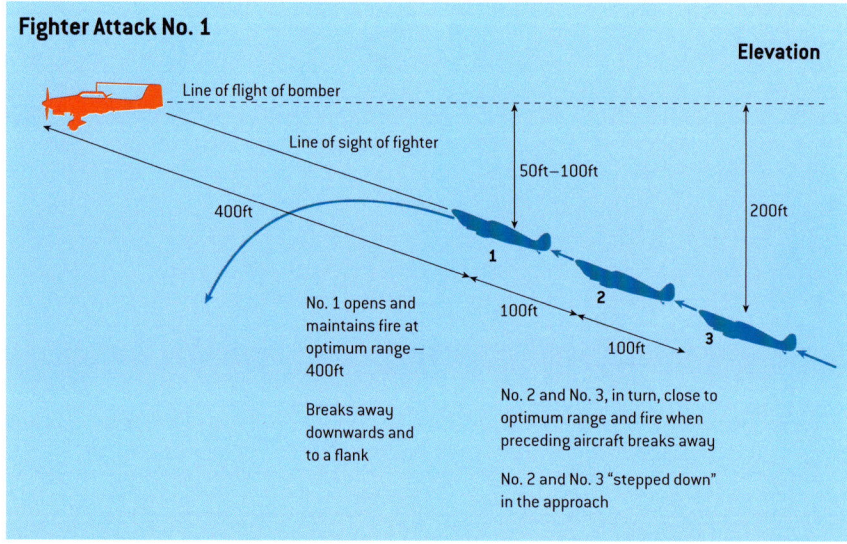

Fighter Attack No. 1

RAF Fighter Command had laid-down procedures for tackling enemy bombers (including Ju 87s), and this is a diagrammatic representation of Fighter Attack No. 1.

Fighter Attack No. 2

Plan

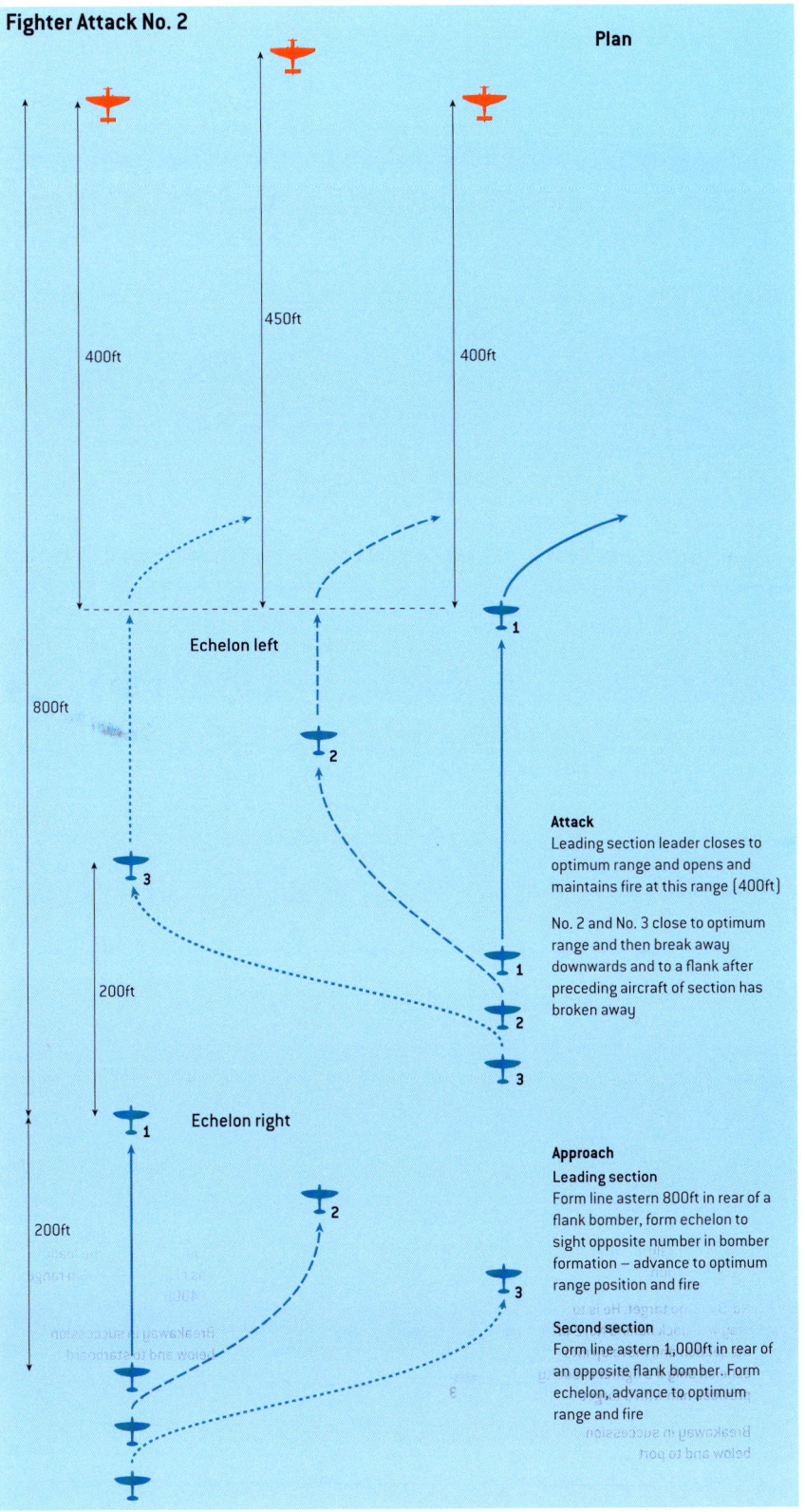

450ft

400ft

400ft

800ft

Echelon left

Attack
Leading section leader closes to optimum range and opens and maintains fire at this range (400ft)

No. 2 and No. 3 close to optimum range and then break away downwards and to a flank after preceding aircraft of section has broken away

200ft

Echelon right

Approach
Leading section
Form line astern 800ft in rear of a flank bomber, form echelon to sight opposite number in bomber formation – advance to optimum range position and fire

200ft

Second section
Form line astern 1,000ft in rear of an opposite flank bomber. Form echelon, advance to optimum range and fire

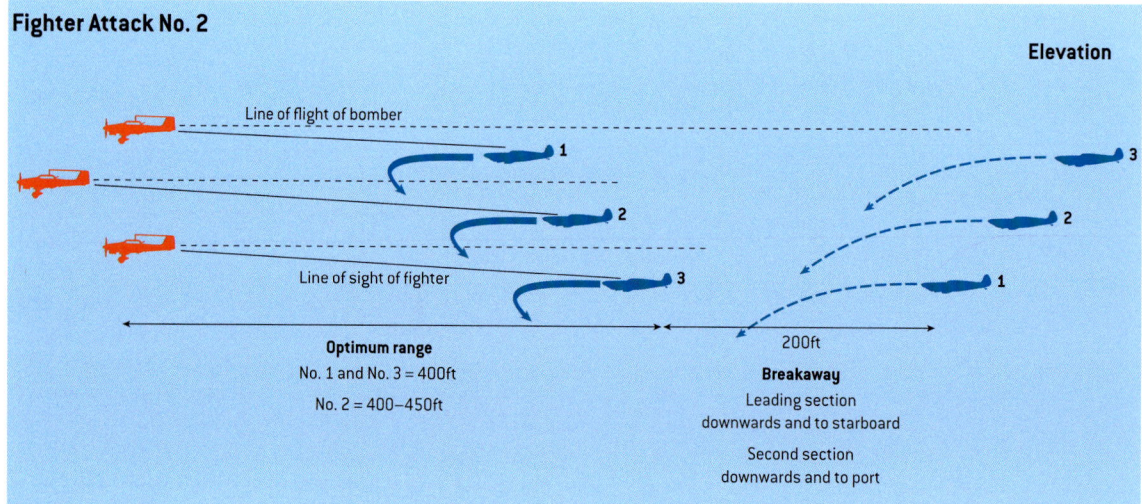

Fighter Attack No. 2

Elevation

Line of flight of bomber

1

2

3

Line of sight of fighter

Optimum range
No. 1 and No. 3 = 400ft
No. 2 = 400–450ft

200ft

Breakaway
Leading section
downwards and to starboard

Second section
downwards and to port

Fighter Attack No. 2

The theory of Fighter Attack No. 2, seen in side view.

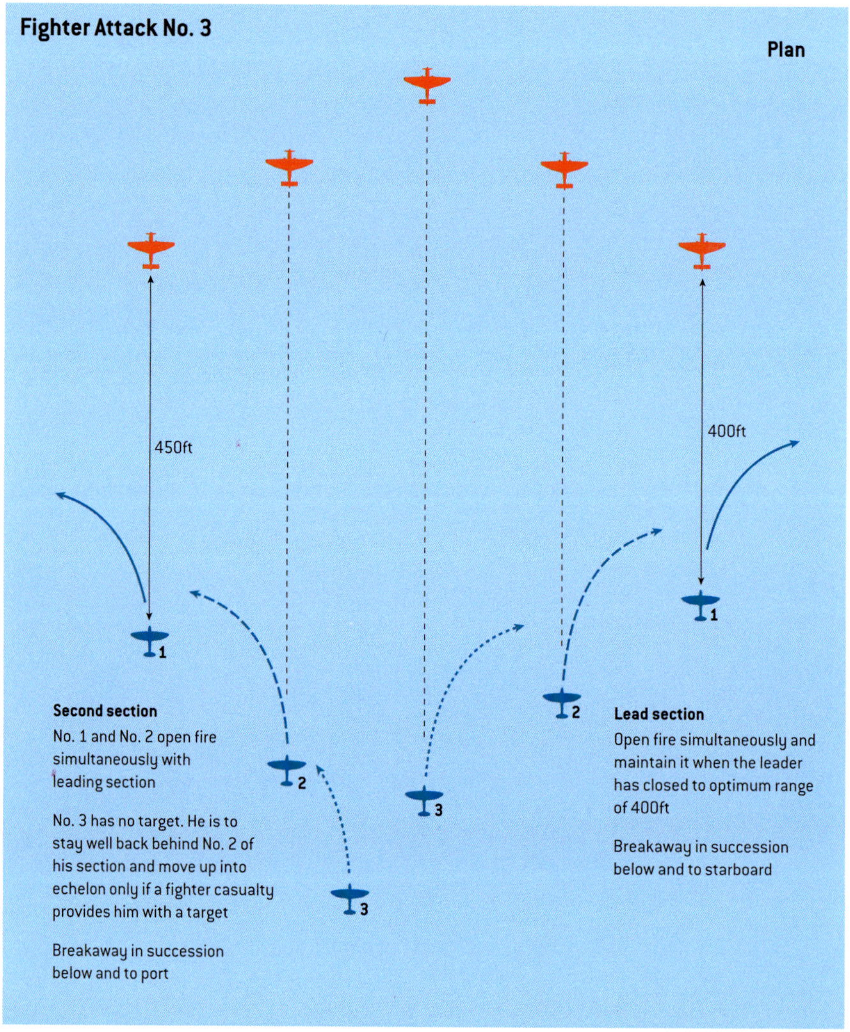

Fighter Attack No. 3

Plan

450ft

400ft

1

Second section

No. 1 and No. 2 open fire simultaneously with leading section

No. 3 has no target. He is to stay well back behind No. 2 of his section and move up into echelon only if a fighter casualty provides him with a target

Breakaway in succession below and to port

2

3

3

1

2

Lead section

Open fire simultaneously and maintain it when the leader has closed to optimum range of 400ft

Breakaway in succession below and to starboard

Fighter Attack No. 3

Fighter Attack No. 3 is shown here in plan view. All were textbook methods of attack that often could not be conducted 'by the book' due to tactical considerations, enemy formations and interference from escorting fighters.

formations. In reality, and when battle was ultimately joined, any strict adherence to pre-war theory was found to be mostly anachronistic. In any event, the Fighter Attack methodology did not envisage the bombers being protected by escorts. And neither did it particularly consider the Ju 87 as a likely opponent that would be encountered in attacks against Britain. After all, the aircraft did not have the range to reach British shores. Additionally, any notion of encounters with the Stuka in Norway, or later flying from bases in France, had not crossed the minds of RAF planners during the early to mid-1930s.

Nevertheless, it would be fair to say that Fighter Attacks Nos. 1, 2 and 3 would still have been theoretically employed against formations of Stukas in the minds of RAF tacticians because these were still bomber formations, and the object was still to destroy the bomber before it reached its target. As was the case with most RAF fighter tactic theories that were born pre-war, they went out of the proverbial window once battle was joined. With the Stuka, that bonfire of theories was, to an extent, compounded by the very fact that the aircraft performed differently to conventional bombers.

For the RAF during the period examined in this work, the principal fighters engaged against the Ju 87 were the Gloster Gladiator II, Supermarine Spitfire I/IB and IIA, Boulton and Paul Defiant and Hawker Hurricane I. Given the right circumstances, all could better a Stuka engaged in combat. Nevertheless, it was not always a one-sided fight, and the experienced dive-bomber pilot had many a trick to throw off his opponent.

As for the Ju 87 itself, the aircraft developed a fearsome reputation during the attack on Poland and subsequent *Blitzkreig* in the West, including in Norway, but its fortunes were turned somewhat during the Battle of Britain. Even then, it was still an effective precision attack weapon, and is often referred to as an 'iconic' aircraft of World War II. Indeed, if any single weapon of the period could be described as iconic then the Stuka is it. Of all the aircraft to see action in this global conflict, the Ju 87 must be the most easily recognisable. Its angular lines, inverted and oddly cranked wings and fixed, spatted, undercarriage helped give rise to the notion that it was predatory.

The Ju 87B-1, B-2 and R saw action against RAF fighters in 1940–41. For Stuka crews and RAF fighter pilots, the encounters saw challenges and steep learning curves for friend and foe alike. Here, a pilot and his *Bordfunker* from II./StG 2 sit on a 250kg bomb as their Stuka waits to be readied for action in the summer of 1940. The collar and lugs that secured the bomb to the aircraft can be clearly seen. (Author's Collection)

The principal RAF fighter opponent of the Stuka in 1940–41 was the Hurricane I. This early example from No. 3 Sqn was lost in France on 10 May 1940, just as the Ju 87 would first be encountered by the RAF. No. 3 Sqn was one of the Hurricane-equipped units to engage the Stuka on multiple occasions during the Battle of France. (Author's Collection)

Strictly speaking, the word 'Stuka' could be applied to any Luftwaffe aircraft employed in a dive-bombing capacity, including the Junkers Ju 88 medium bomber and variants of the Messerrschmitt Bf 110 *Zerstörer*. The name Stuka is a contraction of the German word *Sturzkampflugzeug*, or dive-bomber aircraft. However, even though the name could be applied to other aircraft, it has become the exclusive moniker of the Ju 87.

For the most part, the Stuka was at the spearhead of an assault, taking out armour, bridges, troop concentrations and other pin-point targets. Weaknesses and failings, however, manifested themselves in the aircraft's early deployment, and they would ultimately be exploited by those engaged in its interception. Nevertheless, the aircraft was used through to war's end, in every theatre of operations, and to considerable effect.

Once the Stuka *Geschwadern* were established in France on the English Channel coast during the summer of 1940, they faced not only the hazards of a two-way sea crossing but, for the first time, opposition from a well-organised air defence force with an integrated command and control structure. If the campaigns in the West had, until now, been a *comparative* walkover for the Stuka force, then things were going to be very different over southern England and the Channel. Not by any means, though, did the defenders always have it all their own way. On occasions, the Stuka crews had it all *their* own way.

The fighter pilots of the RAF quickly learned how to best counter the Ju 87 after they first encountered it in action during May 1940. From that point, overclaiming of the type would be extraordinarily high when compared to other Luftwaffe aircraft, although by February 1941 the Stuka's day over Britain was done. However, the RAF's fighter pilots would continue to meet the dive-bomber in Mediterranean theatres, including North Africa and over Malta.

Armourers load belted 0.303-in. ammunition into a Spitfire of No. 19 Sqn in 1940, the unit first encountering the Stuka over Dunkirk and later over the English Channel in November 1940. Although the Hurricane was the Stuka's principal RAF opponent in 1940, the Spitfire also regularly engaged the Ju 87 in the fighting over Dunkirk, in the Battle of Britain and during the immediate aftermath of the latter campaign. (Author's Collection)

CHRONOLOGY

1940

1 May Six Ju 87s of I.*Stukageschwader* (StG) 1 mount a sortie against a Royal Navy Home Fleet formation which includes the aircraft carriers HMS *Ark Royal* and HMS *Glorious*. The Stukas manage to slightly damage *Ark Royal* but are intercepted by Sea Gladiators of 802 and 804 Naval Air Squadrons – the first time Ju 87s have been engaged by British fighters. One Stuka is shot down, its crew being rescued by a Royal Navy destroyer.

11 May Hurricanes of Nos. 87 and 607 Sqns become the first RAF fighters to engage the Ju 87 in actions south of Brussels, Maastricht and near Louvain. In the Tirlemont region of Belgium, the squadrons destroy seven aircraft out of a force of some 60 Stukas from StG 2. Four more aircraft are damaged in an action which, for the first time, exposes the Stuka's basic flaws through deficiencies in speed, armour and defensive armament.

12 May Hurricanes of No. 3 Sqn claim to have destroyed six Ju 87s around Louvain, and to have probably destroyed another two. The Stukas engaged by No. 3 Sqn are aircraft of StG 2, who report the loss of three dive-bombers.

13 May For the first time, RAF Spitfires engage Ju 87s when No. 66 Sqn attack aircraft of 12.(Stuka)/ *Lehrgeschwader* (LG) 1 and claim to have shot down four, with one also claimed as damaged and four as unconfirmed kills. One definite claim is shared with a Defiant of No. 264 Sqn, the latter unit also claiming four Stukas destroyed and two damaged. The Luftwaffe in fact lose four Stukas, with no others damaged.

14 May Hurricanes of No. 3 Sqn continue their killing spree, claiming an astonishing nine Stukas with another two unconfirmed victories. The aircraft engaged were those of I.(St)/ TrGr 186 who reported the loss of five Stukas with another three damaged.

17 May Hurricanes of No. 151 Sqn enter the fray against the Stuka, claiming eight destroyed and four unconfirmed. Seven losses of Stukas by III./StG 51 can be identified as being attributed to the unit, which was led by Sqn Ldr E. M. 'Teddy' Donaldson who claimed two Stukas destroyed and one unconfirmed.

22 May After five days of not encountering Stukas, RAF fighters in the form of Hurricanes from No. 145 Sqn claim three near Saint-Omer, with another four unconfirmed and one damaged. Only one Stuka, from 9./StG 2, can be attributed as a possible victim of No. 145 Sqn, although four others were lost at the same time around Saint-Omer, probably to the guns of No. 151 Sqn's Hurricanes.

25 May As the British Expeditionary Force

(BEF) and French forces fight to hold Calais, Hurricanes of Nos. 17 and 605 Sqns make claims for seven Stukas destroyed, five unconfirmed destroyed and three damaged between them. Luftwaffe records show only five Ju 87 are lost on this day, with no other aircraft reported damaged.

26 May Operation *Dynamo*, the evacuation from Dunkirk, commences, and the Stukas are committed in attacks against troop concentrations, port installations and shipping. Spitfires of No. 19 Sqn claim seven Ju 87s shot down, although their opponents, 3./StG 76, report the loss of only four aircraft. Also on this day, RAF fighters arrive in Norway in the form of Hurricanes of No. 46 Sqn and Gladiator-equipped No. 263 Sqn.

27 May Flt Lt Caesar Hull, flying a Gladiator II of No. 263 Sqn, shoots down a Ju 87 of I./StG 1 in the area of Bodø, Norway.

29 May The so-called 'Glory Day' of the Defiant as No. 264 Sqn claim 37 enemy aircraft destroyed, including 15 Stukas, with another dive-bomber damaged. This figure represents significant over-claiming. Just two aircraft of the *Stukawaffe* were total losses that day, and only one can realistically be attributed to No. 264 Sqn.

2 June Three Ju 87s of I./StG 1 are shot down by Hurricanes of No. 46 Sqn and Gladiator IIs of No. 263 Sqn during attacks against Narvik. They are the last Stuka losses to RAF fighters during the campaign in Norway.

22 June With the capitulation of France, the *Stukawaffe* begins the process of replacing lost aircraft and crews,

repairing damaged equipment and consolidating its foothold in France by setting up bases to operate against the British Isles along the northern French coast. Meanwhile, RAF Fighter Command prepares for the coming assault, having learned valuable tactical lessons in respect of dealing with the Stuka.

1 July With the Ju 87s of VIII. *Fliegerkorps* now established at bases around Normandy and Brittany, an ineffectual attack on Convoy *Jumbo* off Plymouth was undertaken by Stukas of III./StG 51. No ships were lost or damaged, and although three Hurricanes of No. 213 Sqn were scrambled from RAF Exeter, they arrived too late to catch the attackers.

9 July Spitfires from Green Section of No. 609 Sqn shoot down a Ju 87 Stuka of *Stab* I./StG 77 off Portland during an attack on shipping, with both crewmen reported missing. One of the Spitfires is shot down by escorting Bf 110s 60 miles south of Weymouth, its pilot, Flg Off P. Drummond-Hay, being posted missing.

11 July Stukas, with a heavy escort of Bf 110s, return to Portland to attack a convoy. Hurricanes of Nos. 87 and 601 Sqns intervene and one Stuka (of 9./StG 2) and four Bf 110s are shot down into the English Channel.

13 July Stuka action moves to the eastern end of the English Channel with an attack on Convoy 'Bread' by II./StG 1 in which Hurricanes of No. 56 Sqn and Spitfires of Nos. 54 and 64 Sqns intercept the attackers. Two of the Stukas return to France damaged, with No. 56 Sqn having claimed two destroyed and five unconfirmed.

14 July   Dover Strait is the focus of Stuka action, with 40 dive-bombers attacking a convoy during the mid-afternoon, resulting in the sinking of one steamer and two others being damaged. The raid is intercepted by Hurricanes of Nos. 151 and 615 Sqns and Spitfires of No. 610 Sqn. Two Stukas of 11.(Stuka)/LG 1 are shot down.

19 July   An attack on the Port of Dover by seven Ju 87s during the late afternoon results in a claim for one Stuka destroyed in the Dover area by the No. 32 Sqn Hurricane flown by Sgt B. Henson, although no dive-bombers are reported lost or damaged.

20 July   In an attack on Convoy *Bosom* off Dover, four Stukas out of a formation of approximately 20 aircraft from StG 1 are damaged but manage to return to France after being intercepted by Hurricanes of Nos. 32 and 615 Sqns and Spitfires of Nos. 65 and 610 Sqns.

25 July   Stuka activity takes place in the east and the west of the English Channel, with further shipping attacks. In two attacks in the Dover Strait during the mid-afternoon and early evening, three Stukas from 11.(Stuka)/LG 1 and 6./StG 1 are shot down by a Spitfire of No. 64 Sqn and by Hurricanes of No. 56 Sqn. Off Portland, two Stukas of StG 1 are damaged and a third destroyed after being engaged by Spitfires of No. 152 Sqn. A Dornier Do 17M of *Stab.*/StG 1 flying with the formation of 18 Stukas is also shot down by a Spitfire from No. 152 Sqn, crashing in Dorset.

29 July   During the early morning 50 Ju 87s of 11.(Stuka)/LG 1 and II./StG 1, with an escort of 80 Messerschmitt Bf 109s, launch a heavy attack on

This dramatic photograph shows an attack on vessels in the Port of Dover by Ju 87s of StG 1 on 29 July 1940. Four aircraft can be seen pulling out of their dives – one of the points when the Stuka was at its most vulnerable. During this raid, three Ju 87s were shot down and two returned with damage. (Author's Collection)

Dover. The raid is intercepted by Hurricanes of Nos. 56 and 501 Sqns and Spitfires of Nos. 41 and 64 Sqns, resulting in three Stukas shot down and two damaged. Two RAF pilots are missing and seven fighters damaged in return.

8 August   On the date originally designated as the first day of the Battle of Britain by the Air Ministry, three main raids see heavy and repeated dive-bombing attacks against vessels in Convoy CW9 *Peewit*. Eight Stukas are shot down, while 11 more return with varying degrees of damage. It has also been a day of very heavy losses for RAF Fighter Command.

13 August

Stukas from 11.(Stuka)/LG 1 attack RAF Detling, causing a huge amount of damage, wrecking buildings, destroying 22 aircraft and killing 67. This is achieved without loss because no RAF fighter aircraft intercept the raid. Further west, none of the mixed force of Stukas from StG 1, StG 2 and StG 3 either find or reach their targets of Portland, Warmwell and Yeovil, with five being shot down by Spitfires of No. 609 Sqn.

15 August

Stuka activity is again split between the Dover Strait and Portland areas. In the morning, a raid of 26 Stukas of II./StG 1 bomb RAF Lympne without being intercepted, while 24 more Stukas from IV.(Stuka)/LG 1 target RAF Hawkinge and Dover, with aircraft involved in the latter attacks being 'bounced' by Hurricanes of No. 501 Sqn. Spitfires of No. 54 Sqn also engage the Stukas, the squadrons between them claiming 13 destroyed, one probably destroyed and four damaged. In fact, the Ju 87 force lost just two aircraft, with another two returning damaged. During a late afternoon sortie to attack Warmwell and Yeovil, the raiders fail to break through RAF fighter defences, with StG 1 and StG 2 losing four aircraft and having one damaged.

16 August

No fewer than 104 Stukas of StG 1, StG 2 and StG 3 mount a huge raid against targets in West Sussex and the Solent areas, with almost 150 Bf 109s and 54 Bf 110s covering the operation. The formation split up to attack RAF Tangmere, Gosport, Lee-on-Solent and the Ventnor Chain Home (CH) radar station. The latter is put off the air and significant damage and loss of life caused at Tangmere, although

The attack on RAF Tangmere by Stukas of I. and II./StG 2 on 16 August 1940 resulted in heavy casualties for the raiders, with nine aircraft from the unit being shot down and another six damaged. This was Wk-Nr 5618 T6+KL of 3./StG 2, which smashed through trees at Bowley Farm, South Mundham, after being attacked by the No. 602 Sqn Spitfire flown by Flt Lt R. F. Boyd and the No. 601 Sqn Hurricane of Flt Lt C. R. Davis. Both Stuka crewmen were killed. (Author's Collection)

26 Stukas are claimed as destroyed, six probably destroyed and seven damaged by Hurricanes of Nos. 43 and 601 Sqns and Spitfires of No. 602 Sqn. In fact, the Stuka force lose nine aircraft, with seven damaged.

18 August

The hardest fought day of the Battle of Britain sees 109 Stukas of StG 3 and StG 77 attacking targets at RAF Thorney Island, Ford (HMS *Peregrine*), RAF Poling CH radar station and Gosport. Hurricanes of Nos. 43 and 601 Sqns were again engaged, along with Spitfires of Nos. 152 and 602 Sqns. Between them, the RAF fighters claim 29 Stukas destroyed, two probably destroyed and eight damaged. In fact, a total of 14 Ju 87s are shot down, with nine more returning with varying degrees of damage. These losses represent 13 per cent of the Stuka force committed that day.

19 August–28 October

Stuka force attached to *Fliegerkorps* VIII is relocated from the Cherbourg Peninsula up to the Pas-de-Calais area and subsumed into II. *Fliegerkorps* to ready itself to support the planned invasion of Britain (Operation *Seelöwe*) and to train extensively for that purpose. During this period, there are no further engagements with RAF fighters, although 33 Stukas are lost or damaged through accidents and mishaps and many crewmen killed or injured.

29 October
With plans for the invasion of Britain now shelved, tasks need to be found for the Stukas of II. *Fliegerkorps*, so the entire complement of III./StG 1 is sent out in a feint raid towards Folkestone to draw up Hurricanes and Spitfires for engagement by Luftwaffe fighters. The Stuka force withdraws before it reaches the English coast, thus avoiding interception by RAF fighters.

1 November
Again, shipping is back on the target list as Stukas of III./StG 1 attack vessels in the Thames Estuary. Spitfires of Nos. 74 and 92 Sqns are sent to engage them, with Flg Off Maurice Kinder of No. 92 Sqn claiming two destroyed before he is shot down and wounded by the fighter escort. In fact, only one Stuka is lost, probably to anti-aircraft fire.

8 November
Shipping off the Thames Estuary is attacked by IV.(Stuka)/LG 1 and StG 3, with three aircraft being shot down by Hurricanes of No. 17 Sqn.

11 November
Another shipping strike by the entire *Gruppe* of III./ StG 1 sees the loss of two more Stukas and their crews off Clacton to Hurricanes of Nos. 17 and 257 Sqns and Spitfires of No. 603 Sqn, although the three units claim four destroyed and five unconfirmed between them.

14 November
An attack around Dover by Stukas of StG 1 sees the loss of three aircraft to Spitfires of Nos. 66 and 74 Sqns, while two other aircraft return damaged. However, pilots from the two squadrons claim an astonishing 16 Stukas destroyed, five probably destroyed and six damaged. The last attack in any force by Ju 87s against the British Isles, it suffers the final Stuka losses sustained while directly striking targets in Britain during 1940.

24 December
An accident to an aircraft of StG 1 at Maastricht results in the last Stuka damaged or destroyed during operations in 1940 against the British Isles. A total of 101 aircraft have been totally lost and a further 84 damaged through all causes.

1941

15–16 January
Two Stukas of StG 1 are tasked with a night attack on London and another single aircraft with a night attack on Dover. RAF nightfighters fail to engage the Ju 87s and all aircraft return safely.

5 February
While attacking shipping off Ramsgate, three unescorted Stukas of 2./StG 1 are engaged by four Spitfires of No. 92 Sqn on convoy patrol. One aircraft is shot down by Plt Offs R. H. Fokes and C. H. Saunders and Sgts H. Bowen-Morris and C. A. Ream, crashing near RAF Manston. It is the last Stuka to fall on British soil.

11–12 February
A Stuka of 9./StG 1 is lost at night through unknown causes over the Thames Estuary. It is the last Ju 87 to be destroyed on operations against the British Isles.

DESIGN AND DEVELOPMENT

GLADIATOR II

Developed privately as the Gloster SS.37, the Gladiator was the RAF's last biplane fighter, and was rendered obsolescent by newer monoplane designs even as it was being introduced. Although often pitted against more advanced fighters during the early days of World War II, it acquitted itself reasonably well in combat. The Gladiator saw action in almost all theatres during the conflict with a large number of air forces, including some of them on the Axis side.

The RAF used the fighter in France, Norway, Greece, during the defence of Malta, in the Middle East and in the brief Anglo-Iraqi War (during which the Royal Iraqi Air Force was similarly equipped), as well as in a limited capacity during the Battle of Britain. Other countries deploying the Gladiator included China against Japan, beginning in 1938, Finland (along with Swedish volunteers) against the Soviet Union in the Winter War and in the Continuation War, Sweden as a neutral non-combatant country, and Norway, Belgium and Greece, who all used the Gladiator in the doomed defence of their respective lands.

Manufacturing of the Gladiator was undertaken at Gloster's Hucclecote facility, and on 16 February 1937 K6129 (the first production Gladiator I) was formally accepted by the RAF – a little over two weeks later, on 4 March 1937, K6151 (the last aircraft of the initial batch) was delivered. In September 1935, Gloster had received a follow-on order of 180 Gladiators from the Air Ministry, which stipulated that all aircraft had to be delivered to the RAF before the end of 1937.

When difficulties with the Rolls-Royce Merlin engine threatened to postpone the readiness of the next generation of monoplane fighters being developed for the RAF, the Air Ministry hedged its bets by procuring 300 Gladiator IIs as a stopgap via Specification F.36/37, with the delivery of 252 aircraft taking place right up until April 1940. The main differences between the Mk I and the Mk II (with the latter type covered in this book) were a slightly more powerful Bristol Mercury VIIIAS engine with Hobson mixture control boxes and a partly automatic boost-control carburettor. Visually, the most obvious difference was the fitment of a Fairey fixed-pitch three-bladed metal propeller instead of the two-bladed wooden Watts propeller of the Gladiator I.

All Gladiator IIs were armed with Browning 0.303-in. machine guns in place of the Vickers–Lewis weapons combination of the same calibre in the Gladiator I. A development of the Gladiator II, the Sea Gladiator was created for the Fleet Air Arm. The fighter featured an arrestor hook, catapult attachment points, a strengthened airframe and an underbelly fairing for a dinghy lifeboat for operations when embarked in an aircraft carrier. A total of 98 aircraft were built or converted to Sea Gladiator specification, and 54 were still in service when World War II commenced. A number of them saw some brief action against the Ju 87 in Norwegian waters in the spring of 1940.

The cockpit layout of the Gladiator II. The leather straps over the control column spade grip are control locks to secure the flying surfaces when the aircraft was parked. (Author's Collection)

HURRICANE I

In 1934, the Air Ministry issued Specification F.7/30 in response to demands from the RAF for new generation fighter aircraft. Earlier, in 1933, Hawker's aircraft designer, Sydney Camm, had conducted discussions with the Directorate of Technical Development about a monoplane based on the existing Hawker Fury biplane fighter. This had quickly led to the drafting of the specification, which included Camm's preference for the armament to be installed in the wings instead of the aircraft's nose.

Hawker's initial submission for a F.7/30 proposal, the P.V.3, was essentially a scaled-up version of the Fury and it was not selected as a government-sponsored prototype. After the P.V.3's rejection, Camm commenced work on a new design

Despite being 'old technology', the Gladiator II managed to give a good account of itself in some combat situations in 1940. These aircraft were assigned to B Flight of No. 615 Sqn (the last RAF unit in France to be equipped with the Gladiator) at Vitry-en-Artois during the early spring of 1940. (Author's Collection)

involving a cantilever monoplane arrangement complete with a fixed undercarriage, armed with four machine guns and powered by the 600hp, evaporatively-cooled, Rolls-Royce Goshawk engine. The original 1934 armament specifications for what would evolve into the Hurricane were for a similar armament fitment to the Gladiator – four machine guns, with two in the wings and two in the fuselage that were synchronised to fire through the propeller arc.

By January 1934, the proposal's detailed drawings had been finished, but these failed to impress the Air Ministry enough for a prototype to be ordered. Camm's response was to further develop the design, incorporating a retractable undercarriage and replacing the unsatisfactory Goshawk engine with a new Rolls-Royce design, initially designated the PV-12, which went on to become the Merlin engine. In September 1934 Camm again approached the Air Ministry, and the response this time was favourable, resulting in a prototype of the 'Interceptor Monoplane' being ordered.

Prototype Hurricane K5083 performed its maiden flight on 6 November 1935. Essentially, it was still a development of the Fury airframe, with both types being built around an internal 'skeleton' of four wire-braced alloy and steel tube longerons – this structure was renowned for its simplicity of construction, durability and capacity for absorbing punishment. The Hurricane also benefited from Hawker's long-standing partnership with Rolls-Royce, whose newly developed Merlin I engine proved to be the ideal powerplant. Finally, the fighter was fitted with no fewer than four Browning 0.303-in. machine guns in each wing.

The Hurricane went into production for the Air Ministry in June 1936, and it entered squadron service on 25 December 1937 with No. 111 Sqn. The issuing of the aircraft to frontline units saw the RAF finally make the jump from the era of biplanes to monoplane fighters.

The aircraft's manufacture had been eased by using conventional construction methods that also meant squadrons could perform many major repairs without external support from Hawker. Recognising the value of the Hurricane, the Air Ministry rapidly procured the fighter in large numbers prior to the outbreak of World War II. Indeed, by September 1939 the RAF already had 18 Hurricane-equipped squadrons in service.

During early 1940 the Hurricane I evolved from being fitted with the Merlin I, powering a fixed-pitch, two-bladed, wooden Watts propeller, to utilising the Merlin III paired with a three-bladed de Havilland (metal) or Rotol (wooden) constant-speed propeller. Further refinements included the fitting of armour plating behind the pilot's seat and upgrading the wings from being fabric covered to an all-metal construction.

Some of the Hurricanes that first saw action in France were in this unmodified configuration. (Author's Collection)

HURRICANE I
31ft 5in.

13ft 0in.

40ft 0in.

SPITFIRE I

In 1931, the Air Ministry issued the requirement for a modern fighter capable of a level flying speed of 250mph, and Supermarine's aircraft designer, R. J. Mitchell, responded with the Type 224 to fill this role. An open-cockpit monoplane with bulky gull wings, a large, fixed, undercarriage and powered by the Goshawk engine, the aircraft made its first flight in February 1934 but was rejected in favour of the more conventional Gladiator biplane.

Hurricanes of No. 601 Sqn sit at the unit's dispersal at RAF Tangmere in the summer of 1940. Fighters from this squadron were particularly heavily engaged against Ju 87s on 16 and 18 August. (Author's Collection)

Mitchell and his design team immediately embarked on a series of cleaned-up designs, using their experience with the Schneider Trophy-winning seaplanes as a starting point and leading to the Type 300, with a retractable undercarriage and reduced wingspan. This design was submitted to the Air Ministry in July 1934, but again it was not accepted. The aircraft then went through a series of changes, including the incorporation of a faired, enclosed cockpit, oxygen-breathing apparatus, smaller and thinner wings and the newly developed, more powerful, PV-12 engine. In November 1934, Mitchell, with the backing of Supermarine's owners, Vickers-Armstrong, started detailed design work on the refined version of the Type 300.

On 1 December 1934, the Air Ministry issued contract AM 361140/34, providing £10,000 for the construction of Mitchell's improved Type 300 design, and on 3 January 1935 it formalised the contract with a new specification, F.10/35, written around the aircraft. In April 1935, the armament was changed from two Vickers 0.303-in. machines guns in each wing to four Browning 0.303-in. machine guns per wing.

On 5 March 1936, prototype K5054 took off on its first flight with Capt Joseph 'Mutt' Summers, chief test pilot for Vickers, at the controls. He is quoted as saying 'Don't touch anything' on landing after an eight-minute flight. The Spitfire's maiden flight took place four months after its contemporary, the Hawker Hurricane, had first flown.

Test flying soon revealed the Spitfire to be a very good aircraft, although it was not perfect. The rudder was oversensitive and its top speed was just 330mph, which was only a little faster than Sydney Camm's new Hurricane. In mid-May, however, Summers flew K5054 to RAF Martlesham Heath and handed it over to the Aeroplane and Armament Experimental Establishment for service testing. A few weeks later, on 3 June 1936, the Air Ministry placed an order for 310 Spitfires, although the first production Spitfire, K9787, did not roll off the Woolston, Southampton, assembly line until mid-1938. A further order was placed for another 200 Spitfires on 24 March that same year. Eventually, the Spitfire entered operational service with No. 19 Sqn at Duxford on 4 August 1938.

The early examples of the Spitfire I were fitted with the Rolls-Royce Merlin II and two-bladed Watts fixed-pitch propeller. Later, the Mk I had the Merlin III and either Rotol or de Havilland three-bladed variable pitch propellers. Whilst the majority of Spitfires in operational service during the period covered by this book were Spitfire Is, with the Merlin III, the Spitfire IIA had begun to reach squadrons by the end of 1940 fitted with the Merlin XII. The rare cannon-armed Spitfire IB also encountered the Ju 87 on a handful of occasions in 1940–41.

Spitfires of No. 92 Sqn take off from a snowy RAF Manston on 6 February 1941 for a convoy patrol. They are Mk IBs R6908/QJ-F and X4272/QJ-D and Mk IA X4561/QJ-B. The day before this photograph was taken, X4561 had been involved in the engagement which saw the destruction of a Ju 87 over the airfield when the Spitfire was being flown by Plt Off C. H. Saunders. (Author's Collection)

DEFIANT I

In April 1935, the Air Ministry issued Specification F.9/35, calling for a high-speed two-seat day and nightfighter with armament concentrated in a power-operated turret. Twelve companies responded, including Boulton Paul of Norwich, which submitted its P.82 proposal. In April 1937, the Air Ministry accepted the P.82 design straight off the drawing board, ordering 87 of the type.

Fitted with a Rolls-Royce Merlin III engine, and now named Defiant, Boulton Paul's prototype, P8310, made its first flight in the hands of Cecil Feather on 11 August 1937. It was found to be an excellent flying machine without any serious vices. Importantly for a gun platform, it was also exceptionally stable, with its concentrated battery of four Browning 0.303-in. machine guns being mounted in a power-operated Boulton Paul Type A Mk II turret behind the pilot.

The Defiant's turret made it unusual for a single-engined fighter, the aircraft being seen very much as a 'bomber formation destroyer'. Whilst conventional wisdom might have us believe that this was a hopelessly outmoded design concept for modern air fighting, it was certainly not as ill-conceived as has subsequently been noted by numerous historians. Such suggestions inevitably arise from its poor performance during the daylight fighting in the Battle of Britain, where it proved to be no match for enemy fighters.

Certainly, the Defiant lacked forward-firing guns, and had to be brought into a fighting position by its pilot for the gunner to get a bead on his quarry. However, it was never designed for fighter-versus-fighter combat – notwithstanding the fact that, during trials against a No. 65 Sqn Spitfire in 1940, the Defiant 'scored' time and again in a turning dogfight and the Spitfire not once. These, though, were artificially contrived tests for a fighter-versus-fighter scenario, and it must be borne in mind that RAF calculations in the 1930s were wholly based upon the premise that any bomber attacks against Britain would be flown from Germany without protection from escorting fighters. Thus, when designed, the Defiant did not need to fear fighter interference, and the concept of it as a bomber formation destroyer was theoretically sound. Reality, of course, soon overtook theory during the summer of 1940.

In general terms, the Defiant employed conventional all-metal construction methods, but one of its unusual features was the attachment of the light alloy skins of wings and fuselages to stringers and ribs, which were then fixed to the wing spars and fuselage frames, thus avoiding any need to pre-form the skins. Moreover, by riveting the skins whilst flat, this method of construction provided an exceptionally 'clean' surface finish.

The first production Defiant (L6950) was fitted with light bomb racks as per the Air Ministry specification, although these were absent from later aircraft and never used in service. With a wingspan of 39ft 4in., a length of 35ft 4in., a height of 11ft 4in. and an all-up weight of 8,318lb, the Defiant was a deceptively large aeroplane – but then it had to accommodate the turret, which weighed 590lb, plus its gunner.

When war broke out, only three production Defiants had been delivered. However, by January 1940, more than 40 were in service, and orders stood at 135. The first unit to equip with the type was No. 264 Sqn in December 1939.

In service, the tactical and strategic situation for which the Defiant had been conceived had evaporated. Now, in the summer of 1940, Bf 109 and Bf 110 fighters were within range of southern Britain, and bomber formations attacking the mainland were, for the most part, heavily escorted. Thus, if the Defiant was to perform as a bomber formation destroyer then it had to either penetrate a defensive fighter screen or deal with the Messerschmitts when they pounced. All the time, of course, the gunner was reliant on his pilot getting the aircraft into the best attacking or defensive position.

There can be no doubt that without fighter interference the Defiant would have been a good asset for use against bomber streams. The intended tactic was that a section of three or more aircraft would move into a position to one side of and below the enemy formation where defensive fire was at its weakest or non-existent. The theory was simply that the only way for an engaged bomber to avoid a torrent of fire

The rear turret fairings of all three Defiants seen at Kirton-in-Lindsey in early August 1940 are in the down position to allow maintenance to be carried out on the guns. The aircraft closest to the camera is L7005, which was the most successful Defiant of them all – its crews were credited with 11 and three shared victories, including five Ju 87s claimed by Flt Lt Nicholas Cooke and his air gunner, Cpl Albert Lippett, in a single mission. The fighter was eventually lost in action on 26 August 1940 while being flown by Sgts Ted Thorn and Fred Barker, who claimed more victories than any other Defiant crew pairing. (Author's Collection)

from the Defiants was for the target aircraft to break out of formation, thus rendering itself vulnerable to attack from conventional fighters. Theory and practice, of course, were two different things, and the presence of escorting fighters blew a hole in this optimistic plan. However, had the Germans failed to overrun France and the Low Countries, then the Defiant would likely have proved a formidable opponent against unescorted bomber formations threatening the British mainland.

The raw power of this Ju 87B-1 from StG 2 is evident as its 1,100hp Junkers Jumo 211A engine roars into life in France during the May 1940 *Blitzkrieg*. The housings for the sirens on the undercarriage assemblies have been faired over, and later they would be removed completely. (Author's Collection)

Ju 87B-1, B-2 AND R-1

Essentially, there were three sub-types of the Ju 87 Stuka that participated in operations against the British Isles in 1940–41 – the Ju 87B-1, Ju 87B-2 and Ju 87R-1. These were known, respectively, as the 'Bertha' and the 'Reichweite' (loosely translated as operational range), both succeeding the Ju 87A series, unofficially christened the 'Anton'.

The first prototypes of the Ju 87 flew in the spring of 1935, and in late 1936 a handful of pre-production aircraft were secretly shipped to Spain where they flew with the *Legion Condor* in the Spanish Civil War. It was here that the fledgling Luftwaffe gained invaluable experience, testing and refining tactics and developing air-to-ground communications between its dive-bombers and armoured units. This 'dry run' paid dividends, for by 1939 the Luftwaffe and its dive-bombers were ready to wreak havoc in Poland.

It was also during the Spanish Civil War that the Ju 87 acquired a nickname, being christened 'Jolanthe' by Oberstleutnant Günter Schwartzkopff, the *Gruppenkommandeur*

The Ju 87B dive-bomber had been used with devastating effect during the campaigns in Poland, Norway, France and the Low Countries. However, it did not fare well against RAF fighters during the Battle of Britain, and losses were high. These unarmed B-1s from 5./StG 2 are returning from a mission en masse. After approaching their target in attack formation, Stukas generally headed for home in fairly loose groups, as seen here. (Author's Collection)

Ju 87B-1 Wk-Nr 5600 S2+LM of 4./StG 77 was shot down over St Lawrence, on the Isle of Wight, at 1620 hrs on 8 August 1940 during an attack on Convoy CW9 Peewit, the victorious RAF pilot being Flg Off Peter Parrot flying a Hurricane of No. 145 Sqn. During Parrott's attack, the *Bordfunker*, Unteroffizier Rudolf Schubert, was killed and a bullet punctured a fuel line which forced the pilot, Unteroffizier Fritz Pittroff, to make a hasty crash landing. When it came to rest, the Stuka still had its bomb load intact. Carefully dismantled by the RAF's No. 49 Maintenance Unit, the aircraft was transported to the mainland and on to RAE Farnborough with a view to returning it to flight for evaluation. By the end of January 1941 this plan had been abandoned and the aircraft was scrapped.

of IV.(Stuka)/LG 1's 11. *Staffel*, which supplied the clutch of Ju 87A-1s to the *Legion Condor*. Schwartzkopff, regarded as the 'father of the Stuka' (and subsequently killed in action during the French campaign), was inspired by a large pink sow called 'Jolanthe' from the 1934 German film *Krach um Jolanthe* (Trouble with Jolanthe). The 'Antons' of the *Legion Condor* were thus known as the 'Jolanthe' *Kette*, sporting the unit badge of a pink pig on their port undercarriage wheel spats.

Several other variations on the basic Ju 87 design were either trialled or considered by the *Luftfahrtministerium*'s *Technisches Amt*, the most notable among them being the Ju 87C ('Cäsar'). Intended for service on the aircraft carrier *Graf Zeppelin*, the 'Cäsar' was essentially a 'navalised' Ju 87B. Delays in the carrier's construction caused a policy rethink and the 'Cäsar' was cancelled in May 1940 after only five aircraft had been built.

The Ju 87B-1 was the type in frontline service on 1 September 1939, being the main production variant at that time. That year alone, 557 examples left the factory at Templehof, although the Ju 87B-2 would soon go on to succeed the B-1 on the production line. The new version included ejector exhausts, hydraulically powered cooling gills and a new wooden laminated propeller with broader blades instead of the narrow alloy blades seen on the B-1. The B-2 was also fitted with the slightly larger Junkers Jumo 211D (as opposed to 211A on the B-1) and had modified undercarriage assemblies with slightly longer legs and larger tyres. All B-series Ju 87s could carry either one 500kg bomb under the fuselage or one 250kg bomb under the fuselage and two 50kg bombs under each wing.

The R-1 version was conceived for longer range operations and built in moderately large numbers. It was fitted with an additional 150-litre fuel tank in each outboard wing panel, together with a 300-litre drop tank on the bomb racks beneath wing. This increased the range of the Ju 87R-1 to 1,400km – twice that of the B-series.

The B-1, B-2 and R-1 were all equipped with two forward-firing 7.92mm MG 17 machine guns and a flexibly mounted rearward firing 7.92mm MG 15 machine gun.

Generaloberst Erhard Milch, Commander-in-Chief of *Luftflotte* 5, addresses I./StG 1 at Drontheim, Norway, on 23 April 1940, shortly after that country's occupation. The aircraft behind him (A5+H?) is one of the new longer-range Ju 87R variants that saw action in Norway and later along the English Channel coast, where its extended range proved useful when targeting the British mainland at the western end of the Channel. One of the R-model's underwing tanks can be clearly seen. (Author's Collection)

Ju 87B-1 STUKA

36ft 1in.

13ft 11in.

45ft 3in.

TECHNICAL SPECIFICATIONS

GLADIATOR II

The Gladiator II remained in frontline service with RAF Fighter Command throughout 1940, but in increasingly smaller numbers. This unidentified aircraft, assigned to No. 263 Sqn, is being worked on by helmeted groundcrew in an improvised wooden revetment at Bardufoss during the unit's second expedition to Norway in late May 1940. The aircraft is fitted with an early two-bladed Watts propeller as usually seen on Gladiator Is. (Andrew Thomas Collection)

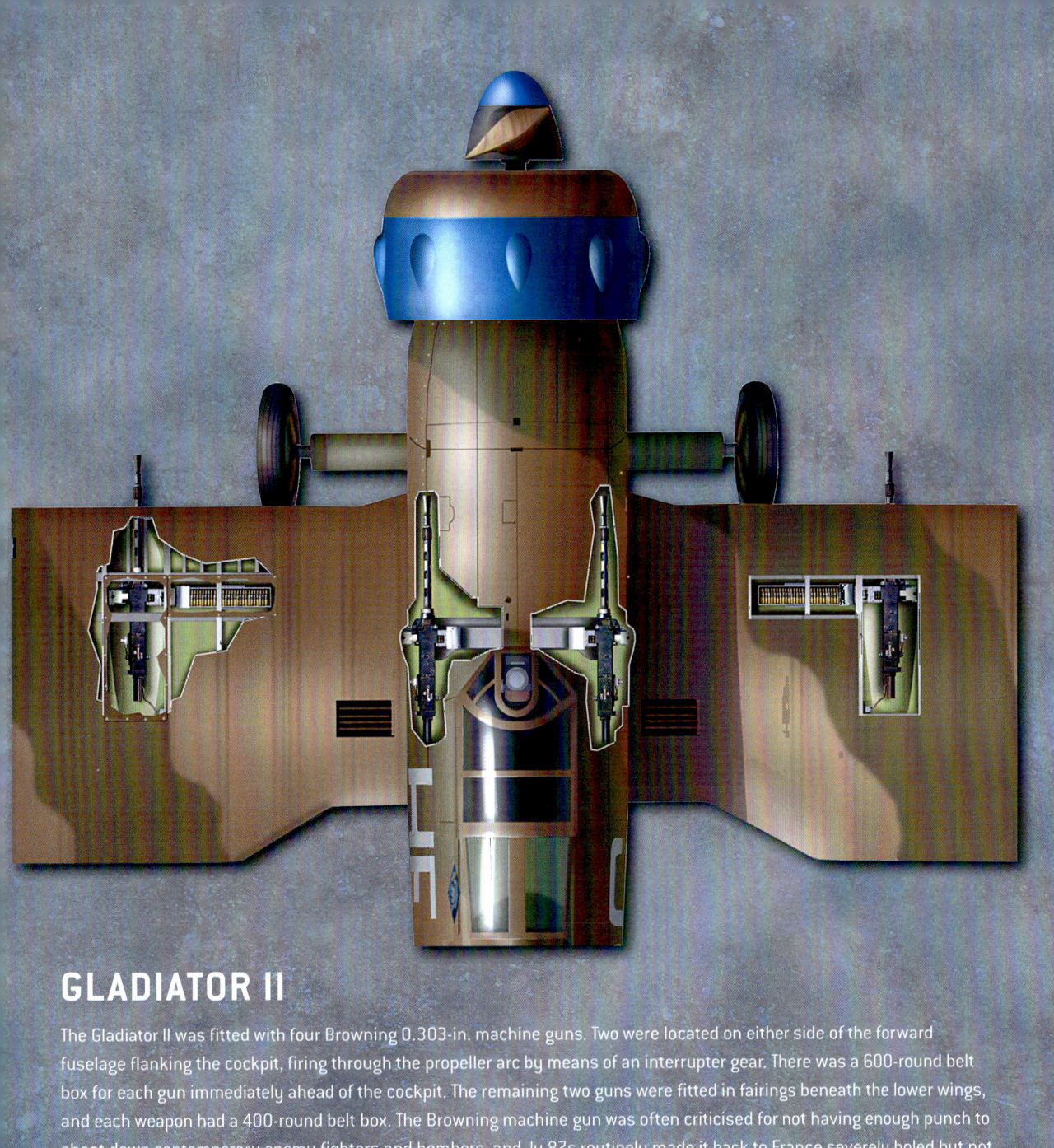

GLADIATOR II

The Gladiator II was fitted with four Browning 0.303-in. machine guns. Two were located on either side of the forward fuselage flanking the cockpit, firing through the propeller arc by means of an interrupter gear. There was a 600-round belt box for each gun immediately ahead of the cockpit. The remaining two guns were fitted in fairings beneath the lower wings, and each weapon had a 400-round belt box. The Browning machine gun was often criticised for not having enough punch to shoot down contemporary enemy fighters and bombers, and Ju 87s routinely made it back to France severely holed but not terminally damaged.

The Gladiator II was fitted with a Mercury VIIIAS radial engine, which produced the same horsepower as the Mercury X used by the Mk I but with the addition of automatic mixture control, an electric starter and a Vokes air filter for service in the desert – 252 new-build Mk IIs were delivered in seven batches, and a number of Mk Is upgraded. As previously noted, 98 aircraft were built or converted to arrestor-hooked Sea Gladiator specification and delivered to the Fleet Air Arm.

Gladiator II Specification	
Type	single-engined biplane fighter
Crew	pilot
Dimensions	
Length	27ft 5 in. (8.36m)
Wingspan	32ft 3in. (9.93m)
Height	10ft 4 in. (3.15m)
Weights	
Empty	3,450lb (1,565kg)
Max T/0	4,864lb (2,206kg)
Performance	
Max speed	257mph (414km/h)
Powerplant	Bristol Mercury VIIIAS
Output	830hp (619kW)
Armament	four Browning 0.303-in. machine guns in wings and fuselage
Production	252 (new build)

HURRICANE I

No. 601 Sqn Hurricane I P3886/UF-K is serviced on the eastern fringe of the perimeter at Exeter Airport in mid-September 1940. Flg Off Carl Davis was credited with destroying one Ju 87 and sharing in the destruction of a second dive-bomber whilst at the controls of this aircraft on 18 August 1940. (Tony Holmes Collection)

Toting eight 0.303-in. machine guns and capable of speeds in excess of 300mph, the Hurricane I was the world's most advanced fighter when issued to the RAF in December 1937. Although technically eclipsed by the Spitfire I come the summer of 1940, Hurricanes nevertheless outnumbered the former type during the Battle of Britain by three-to-one, and downed more Luftwaffe aircraft than the Vickers-Supermarine fighter. Indeed, it is estimated that Hurricane pilots were responsible for four-fifths of all enemy aircraft destroyed in the period July to October 1940, with squadrons claiming 1,593 victories. This averaged out to 44.25 kills per unit, compared with more than 60 kills for squadrons equipped with Spitfires.

Having taken overclaiming into account, the leading Hurricane unit with substantiated kills was No. 303 'Polish' Sqn, with 51.5 victories (although it actually claimed 121), followed by No. 501 Sqn with 40.25 victories (it claimed 101). The latter unit also holds the record for the highest number of days engaged – 35 – of any RAF Fighter Command squadron during the Battle of Britain. Conversely, No. 501 Sqn suffered more losses than any of its contemporaries, having an astonishing 41 Hurricanes destroyed. The Hurricane was also RAF Fighter Command's leading destroyer of Ju 87s in 1940–41, claiming just over eight-tenths of all such victories.

HURRICANE I

The Hurricane I was fitted with four Browning 0.303-in. machine guns in each wing. It usually took a two-man team nine minutes to rearm (refuel and re-oxygen) a Hurricane I, each Browning being loaded with 332 rounds of ammunition, which, at 20 rounds per second, would last just 17 seconds. Being grouped together in a single bay in each wing, and accessible from above, the magazines of the Hurricane I could be replenished more quickly than those of the Spitfire I/II (it took 23 minutes to turn the latter around). The Browning machine gun was very reliable, rarely jamming when fired.

Hurricane I Specification	
Type	single-engined monoplane fighter
Crew	pilot
Dimensions	
Length	31ft 5in. (9.58m)
Wingspan	40ft 0in. (12.19m)
Height	13ft 0in. (3.96m)
Weights	
Empty	4,982lb (2,260kg)
Max T/O	7,490lb (3,397kg)
Performance	
Max speed	324mph (521km/h)
Range	600 miles (965 km)
Powerplant	Rolls-Royce Merlin II/III
Output	1,030hp (768 kW)
Armament	eight Browning 0.303-in. machine guns in wings
Production	3,857 Mk Is

SPITFIRE I/II

The Supermarine Spitfire was the only British fighter to remain in production throughout World War II, and its exploits are legendary. More than 20,000 were produced in mark numbers ranging from I through to 24. This total also included more than 1,000 built as dedicated Seafire fleet fighters for the Royal Navy. Spitfire I/IIs served only briefly in frontline squadrons with the RAF once the war had started, but their pilots were responsible for achieving impressive scores against the Luftwaffe in 1940. In the Battle of Britain, a total of 529 German aircraft were shot down by Spitfires serving with 20 units of RAF Fighter Command. Conversely, 361 Spitfires were lost and 352 damaged during this same period. Finally, of the ten top-scoring squadrons in RAF Fighter Command, six of them were equipped with Spitfires.

The early mark Spitfires were notorious for their light armament, short range and overheating engines (particularly during ground handling) due to inadequate cooling. However, many of the pilots who flew Mk Is and IIs regarded these first production machines as the best handling of the entire breed due to their excellent power-to-weight ratio and beautifully harmonised flying controls.

SPITFIRE I/IIA

The Spitfire I/IIA was armed with four Browning 0.303-in. machine guns in each wing, this weapons fit being given the A-type wing designation with the advent of the cannon-armed Spitfire IB. Rate of fire was 20 rounds per second per gun (160 rounds per second overall), and each cartridge fired ball, armour-piercing, tracer or incendiary bullets weighing 11.3 grams at 2,430ft per second. Total weight of projectiles fired was four pounds per second. Ammunition capacity (300 rounds per gun) was enough for 16 seconds of continuous firing in the Spitfire.

Spitfire I K9906/FZ-L, flown by future high-scoring ace Flg Off R. R. S. Tuck, leads a flight of six fighters from No. 65 Sqn on a training flight from Hornchurch in the early summer of 1939. Following subsequent service with No. 64 Sqn in April–May 1940, K9906 spent time with RAF Flying Training Command prior to being converted into a Spitfire PR III Type C in February 1942. (Tony Holmes Collection)

SPITFIRE IB

Whilst the Spitfire I/II was armed with four Browning 0.303-in. machine guns in each wing, the Spitfire IB (of which only 30 were built) was essentially a Mk I but with a 'B' type wing. This was structurally a Spitfire I wing modified to carry a single 20mm Hispano cannon per wing to replace the two inner 0.303-in. machine guns. The underwing landing lamp was repositioned, with the cannon installed in the innermost machine gun bay and the second of the innermost guns deleted. The area where the inner gun ammunition trays had been located, outboard of the cannon, was converted to accommodate the 60-round magazine for the cannon, the upper and lower wing skins incorporating blisters for the ammunition drum. The remaining outer pairs of 0.303-in. weapons were not changed, and had 350 rounds per gun. Alloy ailerons were standard on this wing type.

Spitfire IA Specification	
Type	single-engined monoplane fighter
Crew	pilot
Dimensions	
Length	29ft 11in. (9.12m)
Wingspan	36ft 10in. (11.23m)
Height	11ft 5in. (3.48m)
Weights	
Empty	4,810lb (2,182kg)
Loaded Weight	5,844lb (2,651kg)
Performance	
Max speed	355mph (571km/h)
Range	575 miles (925 km)
Powerplant	Rolls-Royce Merlin II/III
Output	1,030hp (768kW)
Armament	eight Browning 0.303-in. machine guns
Production	1,567 Mk IA/Bs and 921 Mk IIA/Bs

No. 264 Sqn Defiant I N1535/ PS-A, assigned to unit CO Sqn Ldr P. A. Hunter, leads a tight formation in late July 1940 during a training sortie from Kirton-in-Lindsey. Hunter was lost in this aircraft whilst chasing a Ju 88 over the Channel on 24 August. Airman gunners strapped into the cramped Boulton Paul Type A Mk II turret fitted to the Defiant claimed 15 Stukas shot down, although only two were destroyed. The difficulty of fighting within the turret, the visual restrictions it imposed on the gunner and the disorientation he experienced with the manoeuvring of the aircraft while in combat undoubtedly played their part when it came to the overclaiming of victories. (Tony Holmes Collection)

DEFIANT I

Entering squadron service in December 1939, the Defiant initially proved to be very successful in its designated role of bomber destroyer, especially when deployed in mixed formations with single-seat fighters in support. The aeroplane was less effective against enemy fighters, except if attacked from above and behind. Otherwise, the Defiant proved to be an easy target for the Bf 109E, with 14 having been lost by No. 264 Sqn during Operation *Dynamo*. By the end of the Dunkirk evacuation, No. 141 Sqn had also been formed with the Defiant. Flying from RAF West Malling, it served with No. 11 Group from 3 June until 21 July, when it was withdrawn after suffering heavy losses to Bf 109s in its first action on 15 July. Having made good its *Dynamo* losses, No. 264 Sqn only lasted six days in the frontline upon its return to RAF Hornchurch, in No. 11 Group, in late August 1940.

Defiant I Specification	
Type	single-engined monoplane fighter
Crew	pilot and turret gunner
Dimensions	
Length	35ft 4in. (10.77m)
Wingspan	39ft 4in. (12.00m)
Height	12ft 2in. (3.70m)
Weights	
Empty	6,078lb (2,757kg)
Max T/O	8,318lb (3,773kg)
Performance	
Max speed	304mph (489km/h)
Range	65 miles (748 km)
Powerplant	Rolls-Royce Merlin III
Output	1,030hp (768kW)
Armament	four Browning 0.303-in. machine guns in dorsal turret
Production	723 Mk Is

Ju 87B/R STUKA

One of the most feared weapons of the early war years, the Ju 87 struck terror into the hearts of those unfortunate enough to be on the ground beneath it. Dubbed the Stuka (an abbreviation of *Stürzkampfflugzeug* – dive-bomber aircraft), the prototype had first flown in late 1935 powered by a Rolls-Royce Kestrel engine and with twin fins. By the time it entered series production two years later, the Ju 87B had a solitary fin, a Junkers Jumo 211 engine and large 'trousered' landing gear. It was every inch a dive-bomber, featuring a heavy bomb crutch that swung the weapon clear of the fuselage and propeller arc before it was released. Capable of diving at angles of up to 80 degrees, the aircraft could deliver more than 1,500 lbs of ordnance with great accuracy.

First blooded in Spain by the *Legion Condor* in 1937, the Ju 87's finest hour came in support of the *Blitzkrieg* campaign waged by the Wehrmacht in Poland in September

As a fully laden Ju 87B-1 J9+KL of I./StG 1 takes to the air from Angers during the summer of 1940, the *Bordfunker* stares at the photographer from the rear cockpit of the aircraft. This unit was also equipped with long-range Ju 87Rs during the Battle of Britain, as its airfield on the edge of the Loire Valley was a considerable distance from southern England. (Author's Collection)

1939 and across western Europe in May–June 1940. Although Ju 87s badly damaged seven airfields and three CH radar stations and destroyed 49 aircraft during the early stages of the Battle of Britain, more often than not formations of Stukas would lose up to half their number or be forced to turn back before reaching their target after coming under sustained attack from Spitfire and Hurricane squadrons. Indeed, during just six days of combat between 12–18 August, 41 Ju 87s were destroyed.

As a design, the Ju 87 would be a survivor. In a steady succession of improved marks and variants, Stukas were in continuous action from the first day of war through to the very last throes of the Third Reich in May 1945.

Early in the conflict, the image of the Ju 87 as a Teutonic harbinger of destruction was seized upon by Joseph Goebbels and his Nazi propaganda ministry to turn the Stuka and its crews into stylised figureheads of an invincible war machine. The front covers of *Der Adler* and *Signal* magazines regularly showed artists' impressions of Stukas winning the war for Germany, while Karl Ritter's contemporary propaganda film, *Stukas*, commissioned by the Luftwaffe, followed the fortunes of three Stuka squadrons and their crews, incorporating authentic

MG 15 7.92mm MACHINE GUN

During 1940–41, the MG 15 was used by all Luftwaffe bomber types as a flexibly mounted defensive weapon. The MG 15 was also the single rearward-mounted gun carried on the Ju 87B/R during this period. An easy to handle 7.92mm gun that was renowned for its smooth operation, the MG 15 had an open bolt which stayed cocked when the weapon was ready to fire. This meant that the gunner did not have to re-cock it after changing magazines. The latter were of a 'saddle drum' type and contained 75

rounds evenly spaced on either side, with each magazine giving a burst of about 4.5 seconds. Around ten spare magazines were typically stowed in racks adjacent to the gun, and empty magazines and fired cartridges were deposited in separate containers beneath the weapon. By pulling the trigger, the bolt released and the magazine was stripped of a round, which was pushed into the chamber. A trip lever then released the firing pin and fired the gun. The discharge recoil would then push the barrel back until the base of the fired cartridge case hit the ejector and flung it out of the receiver. This cycle continued for as long as the operator held down the trigger, with the gun being capable of firing 1,000 rounds per minute. On some Ju 87s in 1940, a fender was attached to the end of the barrel adjacent to the foresight to mitigate the chances of accidentally shooting parts of the airframe.

footage of Ju 87s in action to lend credibility. Adding to the cult of the Stuka as the 'elite cavalry of the air', a *Stuka Lied* (or Stuka song) was specially composed with its rousing refrain, 'We are the black hussars of the air, the Stukas, the Stukas, the Stukas!'

Ju 87B Stuka Specification	
Type	single-engined monoplane dive-bomber
Accommodation	pilot and rear gunner
Dimensions	
Length	36ft 5in. (11.10m)
Wingspan	45ft 3.25in. (13.80m)
Height	13ft 2in. (4.01m)
Weights	
Empty	5,980lb (2,713kg)
Max T/O	9,369lb (4,250kg)
Performance	
Max speed	211mph (339km/h)
Range	490 miles (788 km)
Powerplant	Junkers Jumo 211A
Output	1,100hp (820kW)
Armament	two fixed MG 17 7.92mm machine guns in wings and one MG 15 7.92mm machine gun on flexible mounting in rear cockpit; maximum bomb load of 1,102lb (500kg) on centreline and four 110lb (50kg) bombs under wings.
Production	697 B-1s and 225 B-2s

A sight that filled Allied soldiers with dread during the *Blitzkrieg* of 1939–40. These Ju 87B-1s, which appear to have already dropped their bombs, are clearly living up to their billing as the 'elite cavalry of the air' in this staged propaganda photograph taken during the early months of World War II. From this angle, the Junkers dive-bombers were indeed 'the black hussars of the air, the Stukas, the Stukas, the Stukas!' (Author's Collection)

33

THE STRATEGIC SITUATION

The invasion of Poland by Germany on 1 September 1939 was the culmination of events across a period that saw progressively worsening international tensions – a situation orchestrated by the Third Reich – and culminated in the commencement of World War II when, two days later, Britain and France entered the conflict.

During the Wehrmacht's operations against Poland, the Ju 87 took centre-stage and struck some of the war's first blows in decisive attacks. Very quickly, the Stuka proved itself for what it was – a precision and highly effective tactical weapon; in effect, the 'flying artillery' of the Wehrmacht. It could work in conjunction with land forces by

Groundcrew from 8./StG 2 prepare for another move east during the Polish campaign of September 1939. The Ju 87 was very much the flying artillery of the Wehrmacht, and *Stukawaffe* units moved forward as the ground troops advanced. The aircraft behind them is Ju 87B-1 T6+WF. (Chris Goss Collection)

attacking troop concentrations, defensive positions, armour and transport supplying the defenders. On the ground, Stuka attacks could be followed up by swift infantry or armour advances before the Poles had an opportunity to repair or regroup. After all, this was very much the 'lightning war', or *Blitzkrieg*.

With their work quickly done in Poland, the Luftwaffe's Stuka force would be readied for action in France, Norway, Belgium, the Netherlands and Luxembourg. Ultimately, too, in actions directed against the British Isles.

After the *Blitzkrieg* in the West and evacuation from France, Britain faced a perilous situation. Clearly, Germany's intent was to either militarily neutralise or occupy the British Isles. The key to any such plan was the achievement of air superiority over the RAF. To ensure this, almost the entire fighting strength of the Luftwaffe was moved into position on the occupied coastlines of Western Europe facing Britain. Those forces were organised into *Luftflotten* 2, 3 and 5, with offensive operations against Britain beginning in earnest during late June 1940. Broadly speaking, these forces were based in northeastern France, Belgium and the Netherlands (*Luftflotte* 2), northwestern France (*Luftflotte* 3) and Norway (*Luftflotte* 5), respectively.

Although the Luftwaffe lacked long-range heavy bombers, its huge force of medium bombers was now within easy range of all parts of the British Isles, while its Ju 87s could reach key targets around London and southeast England. The latter were also within range of escort fighters that could offer protection to the bomber force. For the Stuka, that was a vital component to the opening air campaign.

In Poland, as in Norway, France and the Low Countries, the Ju 87 crews did not face 'organised' fighter opposition in the sense of integrated air defence command-and-control systems. That is not to say, however, that the fighter defences in Poland and France were *entirely* ineffectual. Indeed, both the French and Polish air forces managed to give a good account of themselves – and particularly so when they encountered Luftwaffe bombers, including the Stuka. However, they were largely hamstrung by having no centralised control organisation such as that which existed for RAF Fighter Command. This meant that encounters with enemy aircraft were often a matter of chance when they were intercepted by standing patrols.

When RAF fighter squadrons operated in France during 1940, they too were disadvantaged by the lack of any system comparable to that which then existed in the British Isles. Indeed, encounters with the enemy were often through standing patrols or a 'best guess' as to where the Luftwaffe might next appear. Sometimes, a frantic telephone call to an RAF fighter airfield might alert squadrons to enemy air activity in a certain sector, but the German aircraft had often gone by the time the fighters arrived. Nevertheless, RAF pilots managed to achieve a creditable degree of success operating in this manner.

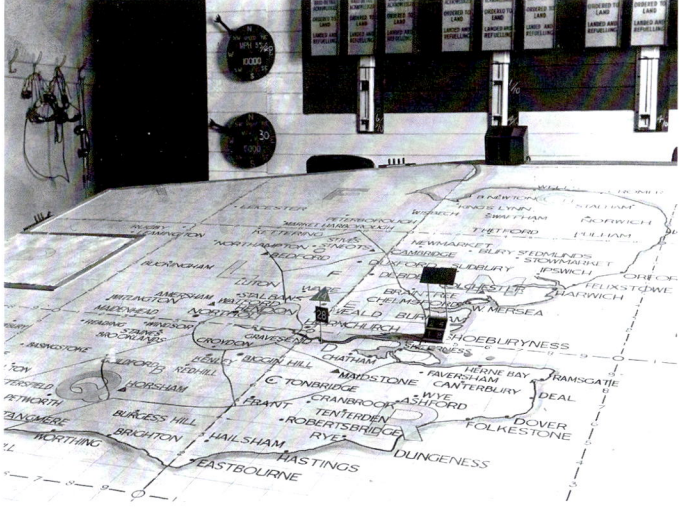

When RAF fighters engaged Ju 87s over Britain, the defenders had the advantage of an integrated air defence command-and-control system to guide them onto raid plots. This is the General Situation Map at HQ No. 11 Group, Fighter Command, RAF Uxbridge, in 1940. Using this map, controllers could see the overall battle situation as markers were moved around the table. In France and Norway, no such system existed to guide the RAF's fighters. (Author's Collection)

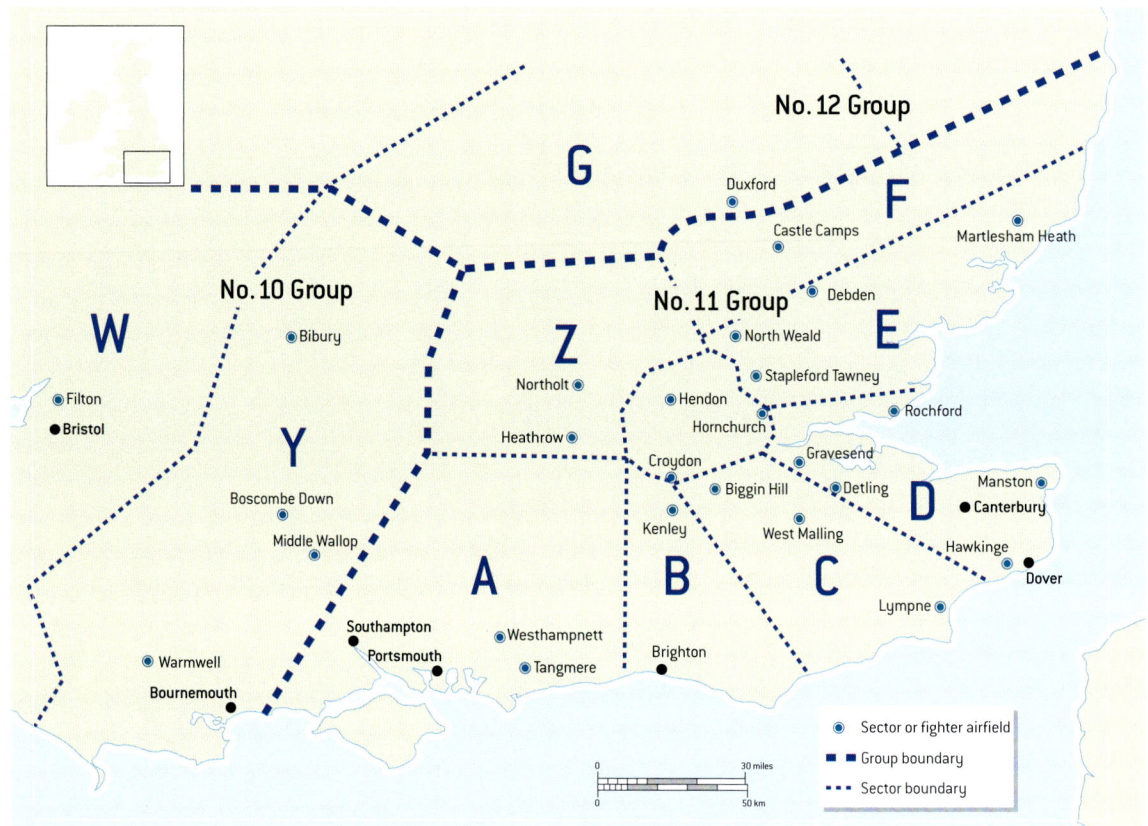

No. 12 Group

No. 10 Group

No. 11 Group

G · Duxford
· Castle Camps
F · Martlesham Heath
· Debden
E
W · Bibury
Z · North Weald
Northolt · · Stapleford Tawney
· Filton · Hendon · Rochford
● Bristol · Heathrow · Hornchurch
Y Croydon · Gravesend
Boscombe Down · · Biggin Hill · Detling · Manston
Middle Wallop · Kenley · West Malling ● Canterbury
A B · Hawkinge
C · Dover
Lympne · · Lynpne
Southampton · Westhampnett · Brighton
Portsmouth · Tangmere
· Warmwell
● Bournemouth

● Sector or fighter airfield
■ ■ Group boundary
· · · Sector boundary

0   30 miles
0   50 km

RAF Fighter Command sector and fighter airfields in southeast and southern England during the Battle of Britain.

The situation in Norway was broadly similar, and over the beaches of Dunkirk, too, the RAF's fighters had no means by which they could be directed onto the enemy. Again, there was reliance on standing patrols, with those at the time of *Dynamo* being flown from airfields in Britain. This was beyond the range of home stations to communicate with the fighters through their TR9D wireless sets. Thus, engagements were mostly down to chance. In turn, this created animosity from the British Army and Royal Navy who could not understand why the RAF was only seemingly infrequently overhead to counter Luftwaffe attacks. The reasons were largely due to operational and technical practicalities. Things would be different, though, once the air campaign moved to British skies after the withdrawal of the BEF from the European mainland.

Although British pilots had gained knowledge and experience in dealing with German bombers during the *Blitzkrieg* across Europe, RAF Fighter Command was now facing a more serious test. Furthermore, it had lost 500 aircraft (mostly Hurricanes) during the fighting in France, the Low Countries and over Norway. In France alone, the RAF had lost 453 fighters, with 534 pilots killed, missing, wounded or captured.

However, RAF fighter pilots now had two distinct advantages over the Luftwaffe to help offset numerical disadvantage. Firstly, they were fighting over home territory, with no risk of capture if shot down. Secondly, they were fighting within an integrated air defence system (known as the 'Dowding System') providing a command-and-control structure which was missing in France and the Low Countries.

RAF Fighter Command was organised into Nos. 10, 11, 12 and 13 Groups during the Battle of Britain, and it faced the Luftwaffe with 644 frontline fighters formed into 71 operational squadrons and units (including two Fleet Air Arm squadrons) when the battle was officially deemed to have begun on 10 July 1940.

The backbone of the 'Dowding System' were 48 radar stations, in place by July 1940, within a CH and Chain Home Low (CHL) system stretching from the Shetland Islands to the southwest coast of Wales. These stations were able to give early warning of the approach of hostile aircraft. In the case of the CH stations, aircraft at medium or high altitude could be tracked at ranges of more than 100 miles, although aircraft or formations below 5,000ft could not be tracked by CH. Consequently, a network of CHL stations was established during late 1939, and these could detect aircraft at 2,000ft flying some 35 miles from the coastline. However, the radar network could only 'see' incoming hostile raids as they approached the coastline. Once they had passed behind the stations, the radar network was blind, although a contingency for this 'blind spot' was already an important part of the system – the Observer Corps.

The Observer Corps had an established network of posts the length and breadth of the country that were manned 24 hours a day by volunteers who would plot incoming raids, with this information then being fed into the system. How it all worked and meshed was a masterpiece of ingenuity, of which Prime Minister Winston Churchill said:

THE RADAR CHAIN AND OBSERVER CORPS' NETWORK, JULY 1940.

A period map of the CH and CHL radar stations around the British Isles as of July 1940. This chain was vital in feeding real time information into the command-and-control system, although it could only look seawards and was not infallible. On 4 July and 13 August 1940, the system failed to pick up incoming Stuka raids. (Author's Collection)

> All the ascendancy of the Hurricanes and Spitfires would have been fruitless but for this system which had been devised and built before the war. It had been shaped and refined in constant action, and all was now fused together into a most elaborate instrument of war, the like of which existed nowhere else in the world.

The information from radar stations was fed into a Filter Room at HQ RAF Fighter Command, Bentley Priory, and from there directly into the HQ Operations Room. Here, a General Situation Map (GSM) allowed the duty controller to assess the threat to each of the groups in RAF Fighter Command and allocate each raid to the appropriate group.

With specific threats allocated down the chain of command to the relevant Group Operations Room (which also received incoming information via the Filter Room,

The radar station near Swingate, to the west of Dover, photographed from the French coast. In this shot, the station is being bombed (probably by Bf 109Es), and barrage balloons fly protectively overhead. This radar station was the intended secondary target for the Ju 87s of III./StG 1 on 14 November 1940, but they were prevented from reaching their objective by RAF fighters. (Author's Collection)

displayed on its own GSM), the Group Controller could allocate hostile plots to the most appropriate sector in his group. Again, the Sector Controller would have his GSM on which all the information relevant to his sector was displayed, and he would scramble fighters on the command of Group HQ, and then control them onto incoming plots. The information available to Sector Controllers was enhanced by immediate information fed directly from Observer Corps posts, as well as information from RAF Direction Finding stations that tracked positions of friendly aircraft.

With this detailed information, the Sector Controller could guide fighters in the most advantageous manner, generally positioning them so that they attacked from out of the sun and, *ideally*, at a higher altitude than the enemy aircraft being intercepted. Although height advantage was ideal, it was not always possible to get the defending fighters to altitude quickly enough. In fact, on no fewer than 30 occasions between 8–18 August, when Stuka operations over Britain were in the ascendancy, the Luftwaffe not only had the advantage of numbers but also of altitude. This was not usually the case with Ju 87 attacks, however, as they were typically flown at lower altitudes than bomber or fighter operations.

The reasons for some failings in the defensive system were varied. Firstly, although the radar stations detected the approach of the enemy, they often failed to make an estimate of height and, when they did, it was frequently underestimated. Secondly, Spitfires and Hurricanes took between 18 and 21 minutes to reach 25,000ft, by which time enemy fighters were usually waiting for them. Thirdly, a controller's orders had to consider meteorological conditions, for he could not afford to risk sending squadrons so high that enemy formations slipped beneath them under cloud cover.

However, the CH system was new technology, and sometimes there were failures – either in equipment, through atmospheric conditions or the result of operator error. Two such failures occurred during Stuka operations over Britain. The first involved an attack on the Royal Navy base at Portland on 4 July 1940 and, ironically, the sinking of the anti-aircraft ship HMS *Foylebank* in the harbour, resulting in a massive loss of life. In that instance, the raid was not picked up by the radar system, and by the time any RAF fighters could be scrambled, the raiders were halfway back across the Channel.

The second instance was a Stuka raid against RAF Detling on 13 August 1940 when a large force, including fighters, went undetected and swept in across Kent,

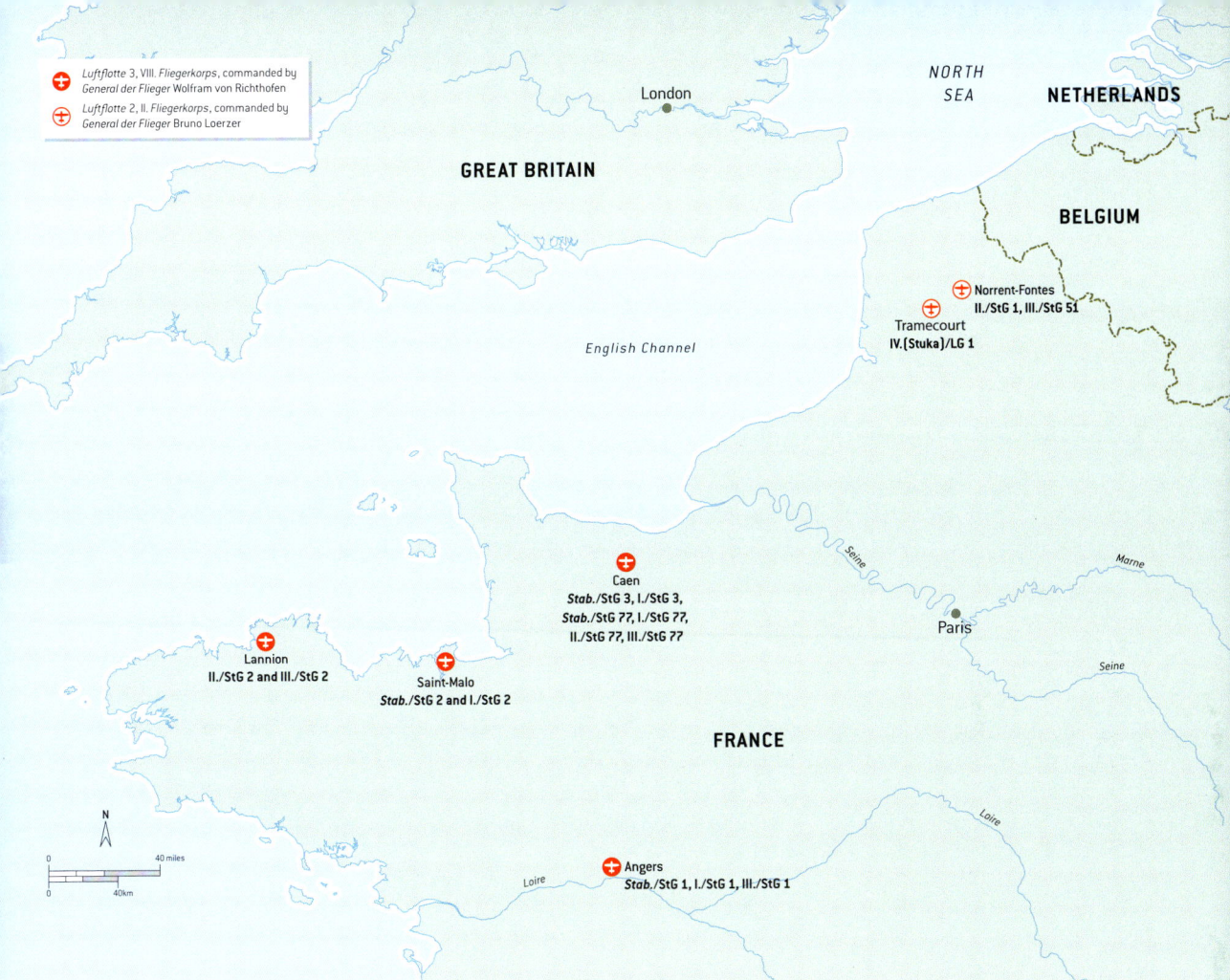

Luftflotte 3, VIII. Fliegerkorps, commanded by General der Flieger Wolfram von Richthofen

Luftflotte 2, II. Fliegerkorps, commanded by General der Flieger Bruno Loerzer

NORTH SEA

NETHERLANDS

London

GREAT BRITAIN

BELGIUM

English Channel

Norrent-Fontes
II./StG 1, III./StG 51

Tramecourt
IV.(Stuka)/LG 1

Seine

Marne

Caen
Stab./StG 3, I./StG 3,
Stab./StG 77, I./StG 77,
II./StG 77, III./StG 77

Paris

Seine

Lannion
II./StG 2 and III./StG 2

Saint-Malo
Stab./StG 2 and I./StG 2

FRANCE

Loire

N

0   40 miles
0   40km

Angers
Stab./StG 1, I./StG 1, III./StG 1

Loire

devastated the airfield and caused another large loss of life, before withdrawing without interference from RAF Fighter Command. Both were unfortunate and costly failures for the defenders, the latter episode leading one Stuka pilot to write, 'The RAF were not there to meet us. Without doubt, here is the evidence that the enemy is defeated and has no fighters left'. It was a different story, though, when the Stukas returned two days later and met stiff fighter resistance.

As to Ju 87 operations against the British Isles in 1940–41, target allocation was handed down from *Luftflotte* to *Fliegerkorps* HQ, and thence to Stuka *Geschwadern*, based on the strategic war aims set for the Luftwaffe at that moment in time. The problem was that Stuka target choices were often flawed in terms of importance or immediate relevance to Britain's air defence. Cases in point were attacks on RAF Lympne (not a key RAF airfield), RAF Detling (an RAF Coastal Command airfield) or on RNAS Lee-on-Solent. None were airfields significant in Britain's frontline defence and were a wasted effort by the Stuka force. It also wasted valuable aircraft and crews. Similarly, so too did 'penny packet' attacks on merchant shipping in the English Channel which did not even come close to closing it to merchant traffic.

In the air war over Britain during 1940–41 Stuka crews would meet determined, well trained and well-equipped defenders who were (for the most part) guided onto their targets by an efficient command-and-control system.

Luftwaffe Stuka units during 1940–41 generally operated with I., II. and III. *Gruppen*, with three *Staffeln* within each group, plus one *Stab* (staff) flight to each *Gruppe*. The locations marked on this map show the locations of various Stuka units (or the areas of their general location) across northern France up until 18 August 1940. From the following day, all the westerly-based Stuka units were transferred to the Pas-de-Calais region to prepare for the anticipated invasion of the British Isles.

THE COMBATANTS

Ju 87 PILOT AND AIRCREW TRAINING

In pre-war Germany, with the resurgence of nationalistic pride and identity associated with the rise to power of the Nazi party, there was a corresponding growth of interest in aviation. Technically, there had been a ban on military flying in Germany under the terms of the 1919 Treaty of Versailles, but this was initially circumvented by 'civilian' flying training, mostly on gliders. When the 1919 treaty was openly flouted by the formal establishment of the Luftwaffe in 1936, flying training took on a whole new momentum and saw not only the intake of men who had received rudimentary glider training but, additionally, trained pilots from *Deutsche Lufthansa,* as well as army personnel and even older fliers from the World War I period.

For the prospective pilot joining the Luftwaffe, the first step was six months at a *Fliegerersatzabteilung* (recruit training depot) which was the equivalent to the Initial Training Wings (ITWs) attended by prospective RAF pilots. At the *Fliegerersatzabteilung,* the main emphasis was on drill and physical training, with the 'air' aspect only being introduced in elementary lectures on the principles of wireless and map reading. Having completed his initial training, the student pilot moved to a *Fluganwärterkompanie,* where he spent up to two months studying general aeronautical subjects

including the theory of flight. Thus prepared, he moved to an A/B Schule (elementary flying school), where he flew light trainer aircraft such as the Klemm Kl 35, Focke Wulf Fw 44, and Bücker Bü 131.

Whilst working towards securing his A2 licence, the pupil received instruction in aerodynamics, aeronautical engineering, elementary navigation, meteorology, flying procedures and training in Morse code. For his B2 licence, he flew aircraft like the Gotha Go 145 and Junkers W 33 and W 44. On successful completion of his B2 training, the candidate had around 150 hours of flying time when he received his *Luftwaffenflugzeugführerschein* (pilot's licence) and *Flugzeugführerabzeichen* (pilot's badge).

Those pilots selected for single-engined fighters or dive-bombers now went straight to the respective specialist schools for training in these roles. However, those who volunteered for Stukas and were selected did not necessarily make the grade, as a higher level of physical fitness, stamina and ability to deal with the psychological and physiological stresses of dive-bombing, including an acceptable tolerance of G forces, was required.

At the specialist training establishment, the fledgling Stuka pilot joined up with his back seater who was officially classed as a *Bordfunker* (radio operator), although he was also required to function as an air gunner. Combined crew training began, flying in operational types of the latest design. On completion of training at the specialist school, the crew usually remained together, having bonded as a team, and were sent to their operational units.

Major Paul-Werner Hozzel was a Ju 87 pilot who led I./StG 1 during the Battle of Britain, and he later outlined the pre-war training for Stuka crews:

The *Bordfunker* in a Ju 87 crew was also its rear gunner. Unteroffizier Heinz Selhorn of I./StG 77, seen here sat on an SC 250 250kg bomb, was one of the survivors of the 18 August 1940 mission – this photograph was taken just prior to that sortie being flown. Selhorn later commented that the back-seaters in the Stuka felt like armour plating for the pilots sitting behind them. (Author's Collection)

> There was initially no Stuka school at that time, but there was the airfield at Barth, in Pomerania, where a Stuka training *Gruppe* was being built up. As instructors, we first had to get familiar, in test flights, with the new weapon before we could pass on our experience and skill. We helped ourselves as well as we could and first teamed up as crews – something which then happened with all Stuka crews coming through training. The pilot and his back seater, the latter also acting as gunner, had to be a real team; one that had to depend on each other, for better or for worse. Hence, each pilot chose his back seater. If, after a while, it was found the two did not gel, the men were replaced until pilots and their back seaters had found themselves. Some of the crews stuck – or crashed – together throughout the war.
>
> After pilots got used to the Ju 87 and learned to have complete command of the aircraft in starting and landing operations, we practised diving. In the vast forest regions around Insterburg [in East Prussia] a bombing range with a target cross and spotting tower was installed for us.
>
> We aimed through a reflector sight, keeping the whole aircraft in the centre of the target and allowing for velocity and direction of the wind, with the aid of the right lead angles. An adjustable red marking arrow was mounted on the altimeter, set to local

Officers from 10.(Stuka)/LG 1 occupy a mix of dining room chairs and deckchairs whilst relaxing with a game of chess at Tramecourt between missions during the summer of 1940. These men, as members of the *Stukawaffe*, were rightly considered to be elite pilots during the early stages of World War II, having undergone 20 months of training prior to being posted to an operational unit. (Tony Holmes Collection)

altitude above mean sea level, whereby the required bomb release altitude could be set. When passing that altitude in the dive, a loud and clear horn signal was sounded, warning the pilot to press the bomb release and pull out. By pressing the release, we also automatically actuated the hydraulic recovery device which aided the pilot, under the heavy G-load encountered in steep dive recoveries, in pulling out.

The normal bomb release altitude was close to 700m. Experienced pilots would also venture down to 500m to increase bombing accuracy. This, however, was the absolute minimum pulling out radius to clear the ground in time. Below that there was no hope left, as shown by the Stuka disaster at Neuhammer when, during a demonstration, a practically complete Ju 87 *Staffel* crashed into the ground because of late recovery.

After pilots had obtained mastery in diving the Ju 87, they practised dive-bombing – first with concrete bombs and, finally, with live weapons – until bombing accuracy was satisfactory. This meant that all the bombs had to be within a ten-metre circle. High bombing accuracy in diving was, in fact, the criterion of the Stuka weapon as compared to bomb dropping over wider areas from level bombing. If pilots did not achieve that accuracy during training, they would not make it as an operational pilot.

For the back seater, or *Bordfunker*, training at radio school and passing as proficient in wireless telephony, Morse code, radio equipment, etc., was essential before he moved on to the next part of his training – gunnery. Here, he was taught marksmanship and familiarisation with the MG 15 machine gun. Once suitable proficiency was achieved, the *Bordfunker* was ready to be posted to the Stuka training wing and pair up with his pilot.

Having both passed through specialist training schools, the crews were sent to *Ergaenzungseinheiten* (operational training units) attached to operational *Geschwader* or *Gruppen*, where crews learnt the tactical methods of the operational units they were to join. As well as being operational training units, the *Ergaenzungseinheiten* served as holding establishments for trained crews until required by frontline units as replacements.

From the time he joined the Luftwaffe until he arrived at his *Ergaenzungseinheit*, a Stuka pilot had undergone 20 months of training and accrued some 220 to 270 flying hours (minimum). He could, in fact, have had more than 300 flying hours to his credit before being declared ready for operations.

RAF FIGHTER PILOT TRAINING

Before recruits selected for aircrew training got anywhere near an aircraft, they first had to endure the rigours of an ITW. For many Battle of Britain aircrew, this meant being sent to either No. 4 ITW at Bexhill-on-Sea or to No. 5 ITW at nearby Hastings.

Here, recruits were put through the paces of basic training – drill, PE, rifle practice and generally learning about the disciplines of service life. Both ITWs were accommodated in a series of seafront hotels, flats and large houses that had been vacated and commandeered for the duration of the war. Drill, PE and route marches were frequently conducted up and down deserted windswept promenades and along a coastline over which many of them would very shortly be doing battle.

From an ITW, recruits would be posted out to various Elementary Flying Training Schools (EFTSs). Here, both theory of flight and flying instruction was undertaken usually on the de Havilland Tiger Moth or the Blackburn B-2. Whilst at the EFTS, the trainee pilot would make his first solo flight. This was typically following seven or eight hours of dual instruction. From here, trainee pilots would move to a Flying Training School (FTS) and, at this stage, they would progress to the Miles Master and/or North American Harvard I. These were aircraft with performances a little closer to the Spitfires or Hurricanes they might expect to fly operationally in the event that they were 'streamed' to RAF Fighter Command.

Should he complete his stint at FTS satisfactorily, the trainee would at last be awarded his coveted 'wings', officially the Flying Brevet, and be posted to an Operational Training Unit (OTU) for final training on either Spitfires or Hurricanes. There were, of course, no dual-control versions of either fighter, and it was thus expected that the novice aviator would first simply read the pilot's notes, be shown around the cockpit controls and then make his first tentative solo flight in a Spitfire or Hurricane.

Instructors at OTUs were generally operational fighter pilots who were being 'rested' from frontline service and, for the most part in 1940, had seen action in France. Thus, they were able to pass on the benefit of knowledge gained in real fighting, rather than what it said in the textbooks. Under their mentoring, at least, newly fledged fighter pilots could be taught the deadly art of fighting in the air by the men who knew best how to do it.

The attrition rate for trainee and novice pilots killed whilst undergoing flying training (at all stages) was significant during the period that RAF Training Command was working at an increased pace trying to keep up a supply of replacement aviators. There was undoubtedly a diminution in the performance of newly trained pilots as corners were cut in order to get them into the frontline quickly to replace operational losses (as well as the toll of casualties from the Battle of France), which were having a serious impact on the capabilities of squadrons in RAF Fighter Command.

On posting to a frontline unit, the pilot would generally first be sent out on Sector Reconnaissance sorties in order to familiarise himself with the airfield, the area of operations and the squadron aircraft. When his commanding officer (CO)

Harvard I training aircraft of No. 2 Service Flying Training School at RAF Brize Norton are prepared for their next flights during August 1940. Trainee fighter pilots would progress to this more challenging type of aircraft prior to moving on to fly Hurricanes or Spitfires at OTUs. Many pilots who would later go on to engage Stukas in combat would have gained experience at the controls of a Harvard I. (Author's Collection)

43

Flg Off Tony Eyre describes a combat to the intelligence officer of No. 615 Sqn at RAF Kenley during the summer of 1940. After each engagement, RAF fighter pilots were obliged to file a combat report which enabled the intelligence officer to apportion claims to individual pilots. On 14 August 1940, Eyre was credited with one Ju 87 destroyed and one probably destroyed. (Author's Collection)

was satisfied that a pilot was combat-ready, he would be placed on the roster for duty and to stand at Readiness – thereafter, being expected to take his place on scrambles or patrols. Usually, this would follow a period of dual flying with the CO in the squadron's Master communications aircraft in order to assess the new pilot's general flying abilities. Once the pilot had been committed to his first operational sortie, it was, quite literally, a baptism of fire. Many new pilots came to their first squadrons with very few flying hours and little experience, especially on type. Some did not even survive their first operational sortie.

A number of pilots were also seconded from different RAF Commands (Coastal, Bomber and Training) to make up the shortages in RAF Fighter Command at the height of the Battle of Britain. Additionally, a handful of Fleet Air Arm pilots also found themselves posted to RAF Fighter Command squadrons. In these instances, a brief course at an OTU to familiarise 'on-type' preceded postings to operational fighter squadrons. However, and despite the overall attrition rate, there was never a shortage of volunteers for aircrew duties.

In the context of training, it is also important to look at what were known as RAF Fighter Command's 'A', 'B' and 'C' squadrons – a system in place from 1 September 1940. The 'A' squadrons were all of those in No. 11 Group and at RAF Duxford and RAF Middle Wallop. These units were at the sharp end of the battle and were generally expected to remain there until the weather broke or the enemy buckled. Some, however, rotated in and out of the main battle area in that period – Nos. 43 and 607 Sqns, for example. The 'B' squadrons comprised the rest of those in Nos. 10 and 12 Groups. These would be kept at full operational strength and support the units in the adjacent No. 11 Group if called upon to do so.

The 'C' squadrons were, effectively, 'reserve' squadrons relegated to the quieter backwaters of No. 13 Group. Here, they pretty much became training units, with pilots often posted to them from OTUs so they could receive first-hand training from a cadre of battle-hardened aviators on an operational squadron that was not in the frontline. The 'C' squadrons could be quickly upgraded to 'A' status whenever required. A typical example of a 'C' squadron was No. 43 Sqn after being posted to RAF Usworth, near Sunderland, from RAF Tangmere on 8 September following heavy losses. Here, it received a steady stream of pilots from OTUs and continued in this role right up until June 1942, by which time an astonishing 87 pilots had been posted in for training.

Although many original pilots with No. 43 Sqn from 1940 had moved on or been killed, there was still a pool of experienced aviators who could pass on knowledge about engaging the Stuka. After all, No. 43 Sqn had enjoyed greater success against the Ju 87 than any other unit during the Battle of Britain. That acquired knowledge was invaluable for pilots who would go on to engage the type if posted to fighter squadrons in the Mediterranean or North Africa.

These were the basic elements of the training for an RAF fighter pilot up to operational standards in 1940. This tuition was all he initially had to equip him for combat with all types of enemy aircraft, including the Stuka. After reaching the frontline, much of what he learned would be 'on the job training' once he joined his squadron.

WALTER SIGEL

Walter Sigel, who was born on 12 January 1906, began his flying career as a civilian pilot with *Deutsche Lufthansa* in 1932, only to then join the Heer shortly thereafter and transfer to the Luftwaffe in May 1935. After serving for a time as a flying instructor, Sigel was promoted to hauptmann in April 1937. That same month he was posted to I./StG 167 as *Staffelkapitän*, the unit then being re-designated as I./StG 76 in May 1939 when Sigel was appointed its *Kommandeur*.

On 15 August 1939, he had a narrow escape during a mishap at the Neuhammer bombing range when I./StG 76, along with I./StG 2, led by Hauptmann Hubertus Hitschold, were demonstrating dive-bombing to Generals Erich von Manstein, Wolfram von Richthofen, Hugo Sperrle, and Bruno Loerzer. Over the range, cloud cover was seven-tenths above 900m, although it was clear beneath it. However, a sudden ground mist developed, but unaware of this, Sigel's *Gruppe* had already started its dive. At the last moment, Sigel saw the danger, radioed a warning and pulled up. However, 13 Stukas crashed, resulting in the deaths of 26 crewmen – 11 of the aircraft had flown straight into the ground and two others had hit the ground during pull-out. The pilots of I./StG 2 (which were due to follow I./StG 76 down) saw what happened and aborted the exercise without loss.

Shortly afterwards, Sigel's *Gruppe* was in action in Poland, where it flew 51 sorties before going on to take part in the campaign in France, where it flew a further 111 sorties. On 14 May 1940 Walter Sigel returned from an operation where he had been wounded by attacking French Bloch MB.152s of *Groupe de Chasse* II/1 over Chémery after dive-bombing tanks to the south of Sedan. His *Bordfunker*, Herbert Herzog, had been killed in the action.

In July 1940 I./StG 76 was re-designated I./StG 3, and Walter Sigel was awarded the *Ritterkreuz* (Knight's Cross) – during the period covered by this book, he was one of 14 Stuka pilots to receive this highly coveted decoration. Up to 18 August, Sigel's *Gruppe* flew a total of six attacks against targets during the Battle of Britain, followed by a further three when Stuka operations were resumed in November 1940.

Following the removal of Ju 87s from the Channel Front in early 1941, Sigel's unit was posted to the Mediterranean and then North Africa, where he was promoted to

Oberstleutnant Walter Sigel in North Africa in 1941–42. (Chris Goss Collection)

oberstleutnant and given command of StG 3 in April 1942. This corresponded with the award of the *Deutsches Kreuz in Gold* (German Cross in Gold). Sigel led the unit for 12 months and was awarded the *Ritterkreuz mit Eichenlaub* (Knight's Cross with Oakleaves) in September 1942. He was then rested from operations. A series of staff appointments followed, before Sigel was made *Fliegerführer Norwegen* (Air Commander, Norway) in April 1944, with the rank of oberst.

On 8 May 1944, during an inspection flight from Vaernes to Hattfjelldal, Norway, his Fieseler Fi 156F-1 Storch struck an air defence cable strung across the Vuddu Valley to protect the battleship *Tirpitz*. The cable snagged the propeller, stopping it dead and causing the aircraft to fall tail first onto a railway line at Faettenfjord, killing Oberst Sigel, Oberleutnant Gerhard Bolz and Regierungsbaurat Gustav Hilburg. All three men were subsequently buried at Trondheim-Vaernes. At the time of his death, Sigel was one of the Luftwaffe's most experienced and highly decorated Stuka pilots.

HERBERT 'JIM' HALLOWES

Herbert James Lempriere Hallowes, known as 'Jim', was born in Lambeth on 17 April 1912. As a boy, he spent three years in the Falklands, where his father was medical officer, before going on to King Edward VI Grammar School at Stratford-upon-Avon. He would later become (jointly) the RAF's highest-scoring 'Stuka killer' of 1940–41, along with Plt Off H. C. Upton, serving in the same squadron as Hallowes. Both men achieved an identical number of Stuka victories.

Hallowes joined the RAF in January 1929 as an Aircraft Apprentice, training at Halton and passing out from there in December 1931 as a Metal Rigger. Subsequently selected for pilot training in 1934, he eventually joined No. 43 Sqn at Tangmere in August 1936 as a sergeant pilot flying the Hawker Fury. Still serving with the unit upon the outbreak of war, but now flying Hurricanes, Hallowes shared in the destruction of a Heinkel He 111 on 3 February 1940, this being the first enemy aircraft to crash on English soil in World War II. On 4 April he attacked another He 111 which then belly-landed on the aerodrome at RAF Wick.

Near Dunkirk, on 1 June, Hallowes destroyed a Bf 110 and two Bf 109s and damaged a third. On the 7th his Hurricane was set alight in combat, and as he was about to bail out a Bf 109 overtook him and Hallowes reportedly stayed in his seat, shot down the enemy fighter and then took to his parachute, dislocating his ankle upon landing. Prior to being taken to hospital, Hallowes was told by soldiers who came to his aid that the Bf 109 had crashed. Having been returned to England, he immediately rejoined No. 43 Sqn.

On 8 August, during Stuka attacks on shipping in the English Channel, Hallowes claimed two escorting Bf 109s destroyed, then on the 13th a Ju 88 and a Do 17 destroyed, another Ju 88 probably destroyed and one damaged, and on the 15th a Ju 88 probably destroyed. He embarked on his brief but successful 'Stuka killing' spree on 16 August, with three Ju 87s destroyed during an attack on his airfield at Tangmere. Then, on the 18th, he shot down another three Stukas. Hallowes went on to destroy an He 111 and shared another on 26 August, his last victories during the Battle of Britain.

Awarded the Distinguished Flying Medal (DFM) and Bar, gazetted on 6 September 1940, Hallowes was commissioned that same month. On 18 December he was

Sgt Herbert 'Jim' Hallowes in September 1940 (Author's Collection)

posted to No. 96 Sqn, then being formed at Cranage, only to return to No. 43 Sqn before year-end. By early 1942 he was serving with Spitfire VB-equipped No. 122 Sqn at Scorton, and while flying with the unit he was credited with a probable Focke-Wulf Fw 190 and damage to another on 5 May, damage to an Fw 190 on the 9th and a probable Fw 190 and damage to two others on the 17th. Hallowes was given command of No. 222 Sqn, also flying Spitfire VBs, at RAF North Weald in June 1942, and in August he was made CO of Spitfire VB-equipped No. 165 Sqn at Gravesend. Leading the unit during the ill-fated Dieppe operation on the 19th, Hallowes destroyed a Dornier Do 217 and damaged another. On 8 November he damaged another Fw 190.

Awarded the DFC (gazetted on 19 January 1943), Hallowes then took command of No. 504 Sqn, flying high-altitude optimised Spitfire VIs, at Peterhead in October 1943. Promoted to acting wing commander five months later, he became Station Commander at Dunsfold. Hallowes stayed on in the RAF and retired on 8 July 1956 as a squadron leader, retaining the rank of wing commander. Subsequently working for the Ministry of Transport until his retirement, he died on 20 October 1987.

COMBAT

The confusion amongst British and French forces in France as the *Wehrmacht* unleashed its *Blitzkrieg* operation on 10 May 1940 would ultimately result in the loss of much official archival material relating to the operations of RAF fighter squadrons then in France. In many instances, Operations Record Books (ORBs) were lost, deliberately destroyed or left incomplete in terms of what was reported. Such is the case, for example, with Nos. 87 and 607 Sqns, the first RAF units to engage the Ju 87 in combat over France on 11 May 1940.

Whilst the absence of further corroboratory evidence from the units' respective ORBs is frustrating, it is known from Luftwaffe returns that during an engagement near Tirlemont at around 1530 hrs that day, the two squadrons accounted for no fewer than seven Ju 87s of I. and III./StG 2, with four more Stukas returning to their home airfields with varying degrees of damage. Between the two squadrons, only five definite 'kills' (i.e. those awarded as confirmed victories) can be traced, but this may well be more to do with confusion in recording events rather than any uncharacteristic underclaiming by the RAF.

For the first time, the deficiencies of the Ju 87 in terms of its speed, armour and armament when confronted with the RAF's modern eight-gun fighters were exposed. It was also an impressive opening score for the RAF's fighter force. Impressive, too, was the tally of victories being racked up by 22-year-old Flg Off Derek Allen, a Hurricane pilot serving in France with No. 85 Sqn.

Armourers from No. 85 Sqn unpack boxes of belted 0.303-in. ammunition prior to loading the magazines of the Hurricane Is parked behind them at Lille-Seclin in mid-May 1940. The unit achieved notable success in the days following the launch of the *Blitzkrieg* in the West, with forgotten ace Flg Off Derek Allen being amongst its top scorers up until his death on 18 May 1940. (Tony Holmes Collection)

Flg Off Derek Allen of No. 85 Sqn was one of many pilots who shot down at least one Ju 87. However, his war lasted just eight days in May 1940. During that period he achieved ace status, had been shot down once and was awarded the DFC. Allen's last victory was a Stuka near Ernages on 15 May. He was killed three days later. (Author's Collection)

History has not been kind to Derek Allen, who might be accurately described as an unknown and forgotten ace. He was also a 'Stuka killer.' Unfortunately, he was unknown and forgotten on more than one level. However, in the space of eight days of aerial fighting over France, he achieved a total of five victories, was shot down once, bailed out and was awarded the Distinguished Flying Cross (DFC), prior to being listed as missing in action on 18 May. Derek's fate was unknown for more than 70 years.

Having joined the RAF on a Short Service Commission on 5 July 1937, he trained at No. 5 FTS at RAF Sealand and then joined No. 85 Sqn in February 1938. Allen was promoted to flying officer on 10 December 1939. While his combat reports have not been traced, Allen scored five confirmed victories, the details supplied to his next of kin by the squadron at the time of his disappearance in action noting that he downed a Henschel Hs 126 and was credited with a third of a kill over a Ju 88 on 10 May. The following day he shared in the destruction of two Do 17s, and then claimed two He 111s destroyed on 13 May. His final victory came two days later when Allen sent a Ju 87 from 9./StG 2 crashing into a small wood alongside the Rue du Sart, near Ernages in Belgium, killing pilot Unteroffizier Fritz Urban and *Bordfunker* Obergefreiter Arno Brandt. Urban is still recorded as missing in action with no known grave.

Just prior to his victory over the Stuka, however, Allen's Hurricane (P2818) had been hit by Flak, although he continued with his attack on the dive-bomber before being forced to bail out. Landing safely, Allen trekked back many miles to his home airfield at Lille-Seclin, arriving the following morning. Almost immediately, he was thrown back into the fray, and on 18 May he failed to return from a sortie over the village of Neuvilly, in France. A Hurricane had crashed near the village at the time of Allen's disappearance, its pilot being killed and buried locally as 'unknown'. Only in 2011 did records emerge that recorded the serial number of the Hurricane in which the unknown pilot had been killed – P2555. It was the aircraft in which Allen had been lost, allowing his grave to be marked with a named stone, the discovery unlocking hitherto unknown details of a fighter ace and 'Stuka killer'.

No. 85 Sqn's ORB of the period is still extant, being one of the few to have made it back to Britain prior to the fall of France. It provides the following brief account for the action that took place on 15 May 1940:

Fg Off Allen, Fg Off Pace and Plt Off Ashton failed to return from a patrol over Belgium. Allen had to bail out when his machine was set on fire as a result of unequal combat against odds.

Adding a little more detail, and specifically for Allen's engagement with the Ju 87 that day, the citation for the award of his DFC stated:

Flying Officer Allen has taken part in all combats with Flight Lieutenant R. H. A. Lee, following his section leader with great loyalty. He took part in shooting down a Junkers, and the next day another aircraft of the same type. After his aircraft had been severely damaged by anti-aircraft fire, he did not hesitate to attack a Junkers 87 over enemy territory and shoot it down.

Whilst a limited detail of an engagement by just one fighter pilot against just one Stuka during the Battle of France, it is fair to regard it as typical of actions in which RAF pilots were engaged during furious fighting over the European mainland. However, and as stated previously, the limited availability of archival material makes it difficult to tell the full story of engagements between RAF fighters and the Ju 87 during this period. Less difficult is the telling of the story of RAF fighter pilots and Stuka crews during the later air operations over Britain.

However, running parallel to the campaign in France, other RAF fighter pilots found themselves pitched against the Ju 87 in Norway. The arrival of the Gladiator IIs of No. 263 Sqn in Norway, joining the Hurricanes of No. 46 Sqn during the early spring of 1940, was an ultimately doomed attempt to halt the defeat of the country by the invading German forces. As the situation in Norway neared its conclusion, three Gladiators were detached to Bodø on 26 May to provide cover for troops retreating northwards in the face of the enemy advance. The three aircraft were flown by Flt Lt Caesar Hull (attached from No. 43 Sqn), Plt Off Jack Falkson and Lt Tony Lydekker, the latter a Fleet Air Arm pilot attached to No. 263 Sqn. The three were thrown into action against the Luftwaffe almost immediately.

The next day, 27 May, things started to heat up when 11 Ju 87Rs from I./StG 1, escorted by three Bf 110s of I./ZG 76, appeared over Bodø and commenced bombing radio masts at Bodøsjøen, just 800 yards from the Gladiators' landing ground. Almost immediately, Lydekker got into the air but was rapidly engaged and his Gladiator badly damaged. Meanwhile, Hull and his fitter were unable to get his aircraft (N5635) started and took cover until the main part of the attack was over. In his diary, Hull recorded what happened:

One of the successful RAF fighter pilots operating against the Stuka force in Norway was Flt Lt Caesar Hull, flying a Gladiator II of No. 263 Sqn. Although he destroyed a Ju 87 there, he was himself shot down and wounded in that engagement by a Bf 110. Hull later returned to England to command Hurricane-equipped No. 43 Sqn, and he was killed in action during the Battle of Britain on 7 September 1940. (Author's Collection)

Suddenly, at 0800 hrs, the balloon went up. There were 110s and 87s all around us, and the 87s were bombing a jetty [sic.] about 300 yards from the aerodrome. Tony's aircraft started at once, and I waved him off. Then, after trying mine for a bit longer, got yellow, and together with the fitter made a dive into a nearby barn. From there, we watched the dive-bombing in terror until it seemed they were not actually concentrating on the aerodrome. Got the Gladiator going and shot off without helmet or waiting to do anything up.

Circled the 'drome, climbing, and pinned an 87 at the bottom of its dive. It made off slowly over the sea, and just as I was turning away another 87 shot up past me, and its shots went through my windscreen, knocking me out for a while. Came to and was thanking my lucky stars when I heard a rat-tat behind me and felt my Glad hit. Went into a right-hand turn and dive but could not get it out. Had given up hope at 200ft when she centralised, and I gave her a burst of engine to clear some large rocks. Further rat-tats behind me, so gave up hope and decided to get down. Held off, then crashed.

Hull had crashed at Bodøhalvøya, having been claimed by Leutnant Helmut Lent flying one of I./ZG 76's Bf 110s. It was he who finished off Hull's Gladiator after shots

Sqn Ldr E. M. 'Teddy' Donaldson, who led Hurricane-equipped No. 151 Sqn during 1940, claimed two Stukas destroyed and one probably destroyed over France on 17 May 1940. (Author's Collection)

had first been put into it by one of the Ju 87s. Hull's aircraft was written off, while he was wounded in the head and knee. Evacuated to England, he was eventually posted back to No. 43 Sqn at Tangmere as its CO on 31 August 1940.

Although not mentioned in his diary, Hull shot down one of the Stukas, the aircraft crashing into the sea – Unteroffizier Kurt Zube and his *Bordfunker* were rescued by the Germans. Initially, it was thought that Lydekker also shot down a Ju 87, but no others were lost. However, Lydekker's aircraft was written off and he was slightly injured.

By only a matter of days, though, had the RAF missed further Stuka engagements by Gladiator IIs in France when, during April, No. 615 Sqn sent the last of its biplane fighters from Vitry-en-Artois back to England, after which it re-equipped with Hurricanes.

While operations in France were being scaled back as British and French troops retreated towards the Channel coast in late May, renewed activity was seen by the Stuka force as the dive-bombers attempted to destroy them on the ground, impede the withdrawal and sink the vessels being sent to rescue the BEF. Inevitably, this would see further RAF fighter engagements with Stukas. It would also see huge overclaiming of Ju 87s by RAF Fighter Command, and because of this it quickly became popular lore that the dive-bombers were 'easy meat'. To some extent, they were.

As the German advance trapped the BEF and French forces into a closing pocket around Dunkirk, RAF fighters were now flying from airfields in southern England on patrols and escort operations over the area while the evacuation got underway. It was during an escort mission for three Armstrong Whitworth Ensign transport aircraft on the evening of 22 May that Sqn Ldr E. M. 'Teddy' Donaldson, leading the Hurricanes of No. 151 Sqn's A Flight, spotted two Ju 87s dive-bombing. He took up the story of the engagement in his combat report:

Escorting three Ensigns to Merville, patrolled aerodrome for one hour and on return just before Ensigns crossed the coast between Calais and Dunkirk sighted two Ju 87s bombing from very low altitude.

I ordered the other two sections to remain aloft and watch myself and also the Ensigns. I led Red Section to attack, but before diving down did a quick circle and spotted 12 Ju 87s in close formation (sections stepped up astern). I attacked rear section. After firing burst at left hand aircraft, it dropped its bombs and glided away steeply, engine off. I think it was hit badly. I did not see it crash. I then attacked the leader of the last section and after a ten-second burst it turned over and dived vertically towards the ground. One parachute came out and what I thought was a body. I watched this aircraft crash.

Donaldson's flight had engaged the Stukas of 4./StG 77 (a component unit of II./StG 77) and his observation about the formation being stepped up astern ties in with the formations flown by the *Geschwader*'s I. and II. *Gruppen* in 1940. In total,

No. 151 Sqn was credited with four Stukas destroyed. Unusually, this tallies exactly with Luftwaffe losses, the aircraft all coming down in the Cassel and Saint-Omer areas. The victorious RAF fighter pilots with Donaldson were Flg Off R. M. Milne, Plt Off J. R. Hamar and Flt Sgt G. Atkinson. Again, it demonstrated the vulnerability of the Ju 87 when confronted by RAF fighters, especially if the dive-bombers had no fighter cover.

This was very much the case on 29 May, when the Defiant I enjoyed one of its few effective days with RAF Fighter Command in 1940. Following a late-morning mission against Bf 109s and Bf 110s near Calais, No. 264 Sqn had returned to RAF Manston to refuel and rearm, before heading back over the evacuation beaches that evening. Whilst on patrol near Dunkirk, its crews spotted several large formations of Ju 87s approaching. With their escort engaged with Hurricanes, the Stukas spotted the Defiants and dived away.

No. 264 Sqn's CO, Sqn Ldr Philip Hunter, did not attempt to follow them, instead leading his fighters down to low level so that the dive-bombers could be caught when they were at their most vulnerable as they pulled out of their dives. Picking their targets, the Defiant gunners poured fire into the Stukas from close range. Many of the Ju 87s frantically jettisoned their remaining bombs and manoeuvred wildly to escape, but Flt Lt Nicholas Cooke positioned his fighter beneath them so as to allow his air gunner, Cpl Albert Lippett, to pour fire into their vulnerable bellies, as he later described:

> Two shot down in flames at 5000ft before they had commenced their dive. Remainder of Ju 87s caught at sea level in line astern. On being attacked from below and to one side, they released their bombs, but three Ju 87s were shot down in very quick succession as we flew up the line. All five Ju 87s were in flames and crashed into the sea or on the beach.

Of this incredible action, Cpl Albert Lippett wrote, 'We shot at them and they went up in flames. Their main fuel tanks were between the pilot and the navigator [sic], and if they were hit, they just blew up'. Lippett had claimed a Bf 109 and Bf 110 destroyed in the morning action, and having been credited with despatching five Ju 87s, he then claimed a share in the destruction of two Ju 88s shortly thereafter.

Despite the inevitable, and considerable, overclaiming in such a large and confused dogfight, 29 May 1940 was hailed by No. 264 Sqn as an outstanding day after the unit was officially credited with a total of 37 enemy aircraft shot down. Cooke and Lippert had little time to enjoy their successes, however, for on 31 May the team that had claimed 12 victories in a little over two weeks was posted missing over the Channel.

As we have seen, RAF Fighter Command's theoretical wisdom for the execution of fighter attacks against bombers was prescriptively laid down. Largely, an attacking fighter pilot (in a single-seat type), or a squadron or flight commander, would strictly follow that guidance – at least during the early part of the war. In the heat of battle, however, the following of written theory would sometimes be impossible, or be forgotten. In respect of any guidance for attacking the Ju 87, an RAF memorandum of the period noted that such formations were often a 'disorganised mass of aircraft'. Whilst this may have appeared the case to attacking pilots, the very opposite was true,

Attack formation flown by I. and II./StG 77

and whilst stepped-up masses of aircraft prior to attack may have *seemed* to have no form or cohesion, there was considerable order to it all. And that included the straggling withdrawals, post attack.

Hauptmann Helmuth Bode, who led III./StG 77 in 1940, realised there was a flaw in having formations stepped-up in the manner flown by the I. and II. *Gruppen* of StG 77. With those groups, the bombers were stepped up with the leader at the lower point, and the following aircraft, in three-aircraft 'vic' formations, rising one after the other behind him. In such a formation, reasoned Bode, the rear gunners could not provide the most effective defensive cover since their field-of-fire above and to the rear was restricted by the aircraft in formation above and behind. Instead, Bode instigated a formation where the bombers were stepped *down* and astern from his lead. This provided better visibility to see fighters attacking from above and behind, as well as giving an unrestricted field-of-fire. In his own words:

> We were flying in vee-formations, one Kette below the others, so all of our rear gunners had a good position with a view to sighting rearwards. With the other two groups, the rear gunners were really limited in where and how they could fire. Upwards, their vision and gunnery was restricted, and they couldn't shoot downwards anyway. All they had was a limited field-of-fire directly to the rear when in formation. Of course, a fighter pilot would try to attack from the rear and could pick off the rear aircraft, one by one, without the others in the formation being able to do very much to help. In our formation, an attacker from the rear was exposed to all the rear guns in the formation. Thus, the field-of-fire presented by III./StG 77 was a very serious disincentive for attackers.

> The effect, in my view, was that our losses were significantly less than with the I. or II. *Gruppe*. That was certainly the case when one looks at and compares the overall casualties suffered by I., II. and III. *Gruppen* of StG 77 on 18 August 1940 – the hardest fought day of the campaign, and the worst for Stuka losses. I believed, then, that my own adaptation of tactics was vindicated.

This was an example of a combat leader making operational decisions in the light of experience, and in the face of Luftwaffe textbook formation patterns that dictated how sorties were to be flown. For Bode, experience in battle taught him there needed to be flexibility as to how operational sorties were organised. Also, it is important to note that not all Ju 87 operations had protection from fighter escorts. Consequently, flying formations that offered the best mutual protection was an essential part of daylight operations.

All Ju 87s in these formations (used in 1940) were stepped upwards, to the rear, from the aircraft immediately in front. This limited the gunners' available field of defensive fire in each aircraft as they were obstructed by the Stuka immediately above and behind them.

Quite apart from consideration as to how formations should be flown on their way to the target area, there were also factors that each formation leader needed to consider when on final approach to their objective. On a number of occasions, Stuka formations were led to a position close to the target by the unit's Do 17M (of the *Stab* Flight) to relieve the lead Stuka pilot of the responsibility for navigating.

For an accurate attack, it was important that each aircraft was heading as near as possible into wind during its dive. As he approached the target, the formation leader looked for smoke rising from the ground, or other clues, to give the wind direction. However, the expected wind direction was briefed prior to take-off, so the leader would have a reasonable idea as to how he might need to approach his run-in and to align his attack by taking wind direction into account. Very often, this necessity resulted in the formation being exposed to attacks from fighters whilst over enemy territory for longer than would have been the case had a straight in-and-out attack been possible.

A case in point were the Stuka attacks on south coast targets on 18 August 1940, where formations flew inland for a few miles to the east of their targets before arcing round on a southwesterly heading to their objectives. It was during this slow-speed manoeuvring that the formation was vulnerable, with pilots concentrating on their targets and holding formation.

For III./StG 1, though, there were aids to the keeping of formation, as their commander, Hauptmann Helmut Mahlke, explained:

> The aircraft of the *Gruppenkommandeure* and *Staffelkapitäne* were marked in a particularly conspicuous manner, with the *Gruppenkommandeure* having both landing gear fairings of the aircraft sprayed yellow and the *Staffelkapitäne* having one landing gear fairing sprayed yellow. This was intended to encourage the enemy's fighter defence to target these brightly marked aircraft and spare the younger crews.

As he prepared to attack his target, the Stuka pilot was preoccupied with checks and settings as he readied the aircraft for the dive. These included switching on the Revi C/12C reflector bombsight, trimming the aircraft for the dive, setting the bomb release altitude on the contacting altimeter, closing the radiator flaps, throttling back the engine and opening the vent blowing air onto the inside of the windscreen to prevent it misting up when the aircraft entered moist air at a lower altitude. Meanwhile, the pilot was largely reliant on his *Bordfunker* to keep watch for enemy interference while he focused on his target.

Attack formation flown by III./StG 77

All the aircraft in these formations (used in 1940) were stepped downwards, to the rear, from the Ju 87 immediately in front. This formation greatly enhanced the gunners' available field of defensive fire in each Stuka as they were afforded the opportunity of getting in a clear shot at fighters attacking from astern.

Ju 87B bomb-release

Underside view of a Ju 87B dropping an SC 250 250kg bomb and four SC 50 50kg weapons. The 'trapeze' bomb-release sling for the SC 250 is shown in the down position following the dropping of the weapon. The trapeze was intended to clear the bomb away from the arc of the propeller and any airflow around the aircraft.

1. Retractable bomb cradle
2. Locking pawl
3. SC 250 250kg bomb
4. Pilot's target-viewing window
5. *Sturzflugbremse* [dive brake]
6. ETC underwing bomb racks
7. SC 50 50kg bombs
8. MG 17 7.92mm machine gun

The Ju 87 had a window in the cockpit floor in front of the pilot, and he used it to watch the target slide into position. Immediately before commencing his dive, the pilot rotated the dive brakes to the maximum-drag position. This produced a severe nose-up trim change. To compensate, an extra elevator trim tab was lowered automatically. When the formation leader commenced his dive, the remaining aircraft followed in turn in an agreed order.

When attacking targets with a small horizontal extent (bridges or buildings, for example) the Ju 87s approached in echelon formation, peeled into the dive and attacked in line astern. Against larger targets (harbours or airfields), they would usually bunt into the dive in three-aircraft *Ketten*, attacking together.

When attacking ships, Stuka pilots usually dived as steeply as possible (and sometimes at up to almost 90 degrees) towards the stern of the ship. At around 1,500ft, the angle was decreased to 45 degrees and the Revi C/12C bombsight lined up on the target's stern as the pilot fired his twin MG 17 machine guns. Gradually, the hail of bullets moved along the length of the ship, and when the pilot saw bullets striking the water ahead of the bow, the bombs were released. In this way, machine gun fire aided sighting and kept down the heads of any defenders.

Once the Ju 87 was established in its dive, typically at an angle of 80 degrees, it made an extremely stable aiming platform. Accuracy depended on the pilot holding a constant angle. To assist with this, a protractor was etched in red on the cockpit canopy so the pilot could read off his dive angle. In the dive, speed built up relatively slowly, and it took a dive through 8,000ft for it to reach its maximal velocity of 350mph. When the aircraft reached a point 2,000ft above the bomb release altitude set on the contact altimeter, a horn sounded in the cockpit. About four seconds later, the aircraft reached the previously set bomb release altitude, typically 2,300ft above ground level, and the horn ceased. That was the signal for the pilot to release the bombs and pull out, while the *Bordfunker* took over machine gunning to maintain anti-aircraft fire suppression.

The act of releasing the bombs returned the elevator trim to neutral and a severe nose-up pitching moment returned, pulling the aircraft out of its dive at a steady 6G. Then, as the nose rose above the horizontal, the pilot closed the dive brakes, opened the throttle, trimmed the aircraft for level or climbing flight as required and turned on to the briefed escape heading. For the 'escape' from the target area, the *modus operandi* seemingly had little structure, although there was organisation and method in what appeared a disorganised pelt for home and safety, as Hauptmann Mahlke explains:

The yellow paint on the landing gear fairings of the commander's and *Staffelkapitän*'s aircraft made it much easier for all crews to collect after the attack. The only order to rally was "Close in on the yellow legs!" Crews who flew past the marked aircraft of the formation leaders on departure from the target were threatened with punishment. With these recognition aids, the rallying of the unit was ensured in the shortest possible time (approximately three minutes), even in the case of the most widespread separation of individual attacks. In the case of naval target attacks, rallying and target departure, as well as return flights, were carried out in low-level flight in what we called a "Sauhaufen" [bunch of sows] formation.

Due to low-level flight, a fighter attack from the Ju 87's defensive blind spot (from the rear below) was not possible. The formation was the most effective protection against attacks from the remaining favourable attack direction for fighters, namely from the rear. The last aircraft of the formation was the most exposed to enemy fighter attacks (the Devil takes the hindmost!) since the weak defensive armament (one MG 15) of the other aircraft of the formation could only be brought to bear against an attacker from the rear to a limited extent, and at long firing distances. The "Sauhaufen" formation therefore aimed at ensuring that – if enemy fighters were to be expected – no aircraft was tied to the position as "last in the group", and in the event of a fighter attack the best possible mutual support of the aircraft of the group could be ensured for its defence.

The "Sauhaufen" worked as follows. The formation leader flew at a very low engine speed (200–220km/h) on a return course so that all aircraft had plenty of speed reserves (50–80km/h reserve). If an enemy fighter attacked one of the last aircraft of the formation, it accelerated to full throttle, flew over the other aircraft of the formation and then inserted itself into the middle of the formation, here again switching to low-level flight. If the fighter did not break off its attack against this aircraft, other aircraft of the group behind the fighter came into firing position for the fixed on-board guns. The fighter escaped this situation by turning and breaking off the approach, usually before it had even fired.

If the enemy fighter, to avoid such situations from the outset, changed targets during his approach, his firing became so inaccurate that – apart from very isolated exceptions – it could not be successful, especially as aircraft of the formation attacked during the change of target had the freedom of manoeuvre for defensive purposes.

As is evident, the tactics flown by Stukas on operations against RAF fighters were carefully thought out and planned, for if crews were to survive, they would need every piece of tactical advantage they could find. The forthcoming Battle of Britain would be testing of both tactics and men.

With the collapse of France and the re-positioning of the Ju 87 force close to the Channel coast, so Stuka operations against British targets made a tentative start on 1 July, with an attack against Convoy *Jumbo* off Plymouth by III./StG 51. It was an ineffectual effort against unprotected shipping by the Stukas. Ineffectual, too, was the response by RAF Fighter Command, which was so late in scrambling a section of Hurricanes from Exeter that by the time they arrived off Plymouth the Stukas were long gone.

For the crews of III./StG 51, notwithstanding their disappointing results against merchant shipping, it may have seemed that future operations against Britain would not be unduly bothered by fighter interference – a view likely reinforced three days later when around 30 Stukas from the unit dive-bombed Portland naval base.

During a devastating attack at 0830 hrs on 4 July, the anti-aircraft vessel HMS *Foylebank* was hit and sunk with the loss of 176 crew, while a convoy further out to sea was dive-bombed. Despite the scale of the attack, RAF Fighter Command did not get any aircraft into the air. For the RAF, it was an inauspicious curtain-raiser for the battles on the Channel coast which would soon evolve into the Battle of Britain. They needed to do better, and on 9 July they did. This time, it was the Stukas of I./StG 77 who would have their baptism of fire flying against Britain. One of the pilots involved was Oberleutnant Kurt Scheffel (the *Gruppe* technical officer) who had completed 62 combat missions by the end of the Polish campaign. He wrote a vivid account of the action on the 9th:

> The *Gruppe*, with the *Stab* and 1st *Staffel*, was sent up to Theville, east of Cherbourg, as traffic in the Channel had been reported. Theville was previously a French airfield, and

Ju 87B COCKPIT

1. Fuel pressure gauge
2. Radio altimeter
3. Magnetic compass
4. Cockpit light controls
5. Starter switch
6. Rate of climb indicator
7. Altimeter
8. Bomb window control
9. Fuel gauge
10. Compass repeater
11. Artificial horizon
12. Bomb altimeter
13. KG 12A control column
14. Engine priming pump
15. Oil cooling flap control
16. Supercharger pressure dial
17. Rev counter dial
18. Airspeed indicator
19. Clock
20. Revi C/12C bombsight
21. Loading buttons
22. Test lamp
23. Hydraulic pressure switches
24. Fuel cock
25. Instrument shroud padding
26. Cockpit ventilation control
27. Supercharger handle
28. Canopy latch handle
29. Wing bomb-arming switches
30. Oil pressure gauge
31. Fuselage bomb-arming switch
32. Wing/fuselage bomb selector switches
33. Bomb jettison handle
34. Hand pump
35. Rear-view mirror
36. Coolant temperature gauge
37. Oil temperature gauge
38. Fuel tank selector
39. Cockpit lights
40. Circuit breaker panel
41. Seat adjustment handle
42. Throttle
43. Propeller pitch control
44. Magnetos
45. War emergency power control
46. Electrical lead for Revi C/12C bombsight
47. Switch and test box
48. Cockpit ventilator
49. Rudder pedals
50. Pilot's seat and cushion
51. Pilot's target window

Pilots and aircrew from I./StG 77 relax between sorties at Caen during the summer of 1940. On the left, wearing the white tunic, is Oberleutnant Fritz Sayler, *Staffelkapitän* of 2./StG 77, with Hauptmann Karl Henze (then *Staffelkapitän* of 1./StG 77) sitting in the deckchair. These crewmen were heavily involved in the south coast attacks undertaken by I./StG 77 in early July 1940. (Author's Collection)

quite large. We spent the morning sunbathing next to our machines, but in the evening, the order to attack ships between Portland and Torquay arrived.

We took off with the *Stab* Flight and the 1st *Staffel*, guided towards our target by the unit's Dornier 17. We first flew towards the Portland Peninsula, halfway up the English Channel, with the high clouds having disappeared, giving way to clear skies. Near the cliffs of England, we spotted two small ships of about 2,000–3,000 tons each. They were to be attacked by the *Stab*, while the 1st *Staffel* continued towards Torquay.

The leader approached the ships from the east and then we dived, the leader first, followed by [Hauptmann Karl] Henze, and me last of all. However, the direction of the wind we had been given was apparently incorrect, so the bombs fell into the sea on the right side of the ships. Henze had sunk quite low, and I had to follow him.

We were widely scattered after the dive, and I had to run after the leader who was about 800m ahead and 200m higher. We followed the English coast to the west, the commander in front, Henze on the right and me on the left. Behind my right wing, I could see Portland very clearly. We were now at an altitude of 2,000m, and still about 500m from the commander, when I suddenly saw an English fighter heading towards us from Portland. At first, I was terrified. I was completely speechless. I had to look again to be sure I had seen correctly. But I was right – there were 10 to 15 Spitfires, and they were closing in at frightening speed. Neither the commander, nor Henze, nor the three radio operators had seen them.

I shouted over the radio, "To the right! Enemy fighters!" As the commander did not react, I repeated the same sentence, adding, "Turn to the right into the clouds!" Further up the English Channel, and 300m below us, there was a thick patch of cloud. This became our saviour, but there was no longer any chance us of catching the commander. He was too far away, it was too late and the Spitfires were right behind us. I had just enough time to see how Henze veered south – and that's when the wild dance began.

I was heading towards the clouds at full throttle when the first tracer bullets passed in front of me. Like a madman, my radio operator started firing his machine gun while indicating from which direction the enemy fighters were attacking. I put the aircraft on its nose, pulled up in a steep climb, turned to the left and made a sharp turn to the right, with both hands on the stick.

Long bursts of tracer bullets passed in front of my aircraft and some Spitfires approached so close that I could make out the faces of the pilots. There were about five of them now, and they were trying to finish me off. I only had one goal at this point in the fight – to the clouds, the clouds!

I can't say how long the dance lasted, but I clearly remember the wild cries of my radio operator. "From the left! From the right! Above! Below!" and how he cursed rudely between each warning. The empty ammunition drums from the machine gun were supposed to be kept in a container with a lid, but during the air combat this obviously went wrong and suddenly the empty drums began to fly around the cockpit, causing my radio operator minor head and shoulder injuries.

Suddenly, I found myself in the cloud, and my surroundings turned milky white. I could breathe a sigh of relief, or at least I thought so. But at that moment, my radio operator shouted to me. "Aircraft coming from the left!" I threw the aircraft into another left turn, pushed the stick and got out of the clouds. Below, an enemy machine was heading towards me, firing. So, I went back into the cloud layer, which was very thin. However, the enemy hunters above could see the stream of a wake from my propeller; they only had to follow the whirlwind I was making and open fire. All of this was repeated twice more, then calm returned.

I was able to leave the clouds, and my radio operator stopped firing. I had been flying blind with instruments through the clouds. It worked well, but I was not familiar with this type of flying. My radio operator was not badly injured, except for several bruises caused by ammunition drums that had been buzzing around in the cockpit like flies. After 20 minutes, we calmed down and I slowly descended to a lower altitude to check if we were close to the coast. Everything was clear and no other aircraft were visible.

We had just landed, and I was returning the machine to our dispersal area when my radio operator shouted, "Three fighters approaching from the sea!" Had the English pursued us? I turned off the ignition and we both jumped out of the cockpit, flattening ourselves on the ground. The three hunters roared above our heads, but they were Messerschmitt 109s returning from a mission! It was a false alarm.

The engaging fighters were from No. 609 Sqn, although Scheffel's account of '10 to 15 Spitfires' was exaggerated. One can imagine that the three Spitfires flown by Flg Offs D. M. Crook and P. Drummond-Hay and Plt Off M. J. Appleby had zipped in and out of the formation so many times, and so quickly, that Scheffel kept counting the same aircraft. Either way, the trio jointly claimed one Stuka destroyed and one probably destroyed, although combat reports for the engagement have not survived. The Stuka sortie had been flown with an escort provided by the Bf 110s of V.(*Zerstörer*)/LG 1, the German fighters shooting down the aircraft of Peter Drummond-Hay, who was killed.

The *Gruppenkommandeur*, Hauptmann Friedrich-Karl *Freiherr* von Dalwigk zu Lichtenfels, led the attack, but he and his *Bordfunker*, Feldwebel Karl Götz, failed to return. Although theirs was the only Stuka to be lost, it was a heavy price to pay when set against the mission's sole success – slight damage inflicted on the merchantman SS *Empire Daffodil*.

July continued with sporadic attacks by the Stukas while the Luftwaffe continued its futile attempt to close the English Channel by targeting shipping, with Ju 87 losses to RAF fighters seen on 13, 14, 20, 25, 27 and 29 July. But it was on 8 August that Channel shipping attacks by Stukas reached a crescendo.

1. Seat
2. Control column
3. Rudder pedal adjusting wheels
4. Rudder pedals
5. Radiator flap control lever
6. Map case
7. Oil dilution push button
8. Rudder trim wheel
9. Pressure head heater switch
10. Elevator trim wheel
11. Crowbar
12. Door catch
13. Camera indication supply plug
14. Mixture lever
15. Throttle lever
16. Propeller control lever
17. Boost control cut-out

18. Radio controller
19. Ignition switches
20. Brake triple pressure gauge
21. Elevator tabs position indicator
22. Oxygen regulator
23. Navigation lights switch
24. Flaps control
25. Airspeed indicator
26. Altimeter
27. Gun button
28. Cockpit light switches
29. Direction indicator setting knob
30. Artificial horizon
31. GM 2 reflector gunsight
32. Rear-view mirror
33. Ventilator control

34. Rate of climb indicator
35. Turn and slip indicator
36. Booster coil pushbutton
37. Engine starting pushbutton
38. Oil pressure gauge
39. Oil temperature gauge
40. Fuel gauge and pushbutton
41. Radiator temperature gauge
42. Boost pressure gauge
43. Fuel pressure warning lamps
44. Engine rpm gauge
45. Stowage for GM 2 reflector sight lamps
46. Cockpit light
47. Signalling switchbox
48. Remote contactor and switch
49. Fuel tank pressurising cock control lever

50. Slow running cut-out control
51. Priming pump
52. Fuel cock
53. Compass
54. Undercarriage control lever
55. Harness release
56. Oxygen hose
57. IFF Controls
58. CO_2 cylinder for undercarriage emergency lowering
59. Oxygen supply cock
60. Windscreen de-icing pump
61. Windscreen de-icing needle valve
62. Undercarriage emergency lowering control
63. Windscreen de-icing cock
64. Pilot's seat

On that day, some 30 enemy aircraft were detected off Cherbourg by Ventnor CH radar station at around 0840 hrs. Fifteen minutes later, a formation of equal strength was located between the Seine and Selsey Bill. Already, RAF Fighter Command had a standing patrol over Convoy CW9 *Peewit* in the form of six Hurricanes of No. 601 Sqn led by Flt Lt Archibald Hope. Unfortunately, the Hurricanes returned to Tangmere before any sniff of action, landing back at 0850 hrs just as the Stukas were bearing down on the ships. It was the same story, too, with 12 Spitfires from No. 609 Sqn that were ordered off from Warmwell at 0900 hrs, only to arrive just too late to engage.

The Stukas were also missed by three Spitfires of No. 234 Sqn's Yellow Section that had been airborne from St Eval since 0755 hrs. Vectored onto CW9 *Peewit*, they arrived over the convoy after the enemy had left. However, Hurricanes from No. 145 Sqn, up from Westhampnett, that had taken No. 601 Sqn's place enjoyed better luck. Sqn Ldr J. R. A. Peel had led his Hurricanes off at 0830 hrs, in time to intercept the Stukas off St Catherine's Point – although not before they had already bombed the ships. The Hurricanes found themselves facing a formidable armada of enemy aircraft. Peel takes up the story:

I was leader of A Flight of 145 Sqn ordered to patrol convoy off St Catherine's Point. Received warning of enemy aircraft approaching from SW and climbed into sun at 16,000ft. Saw large formation of Ju 87s approaching from SW in vic formation with Me 109s stepped up to rear at 12,000ft. Approached unobserved from sea and went into attack on rear Ju 87s with Yellow Section before enemy fighters could intercept. Gave one Ju 87 a five-second burst at 250 yards but did not observe results as I broke to engage two Me 109s. These fought by half rolling, diving and zooming in climbing turns. Got on tail of one Me 109 and gave him two five-second bursts at 100 yards. Smoke came from starboard wing, and he dived to south at sea level. Followed second Me 109 up in a zoom and caught him with a deflection shot at the stall. Enemy aircraft immediately dived to sea level and made off at fifty feet. Gave chase for three minutes but unable to close up enough for effective shooting.

Turned back towards engagement and found about twenty Ju 87s flying southwards at about 1,000ft in a vic on my beam. Attacked one straggler and shot him down into the sea. Me 109 then carried out a beam attack but didn't give enough deflection. Attacked another Ju 87 some distance behind with a beam attack but my guns stopped after a two-second burst. Enemy aircraft dropped to sea level and flew off in a right hand turn very unsteadily and appeared badly damaged.

By the end of the day, three individual Stuka attacks had taken place against the convoy involving aircraft of StG 1, StG 2, StG 3 and StG 77. Between them, the four units had lost eight aircraft, with others damaged and crew members wounded.

RAF Fighter Command had lost at least ten aircraft during the battle against the Stukas, although overclaiming

The rear cockpit of the 4./StG 77 Ju 87B-1 downed by Flg Off Parrott of No. 145 Sqn on 8 August 1940. The pilot of the dive-bomber, Unteroffizier Fritz Pittrof, was captured unhurt, while his *Bordfunker*, Unteroffizier Rudlof Schubert, was killed in the attack by the Hurricane. The cylindrical objects in the lower foreground are fluorescein dye packets to mark the water for air-sea rescue purposes should the aircraft have come down in the sea. The spatters on the Perspex are blood spray from the unfortunate Unteroffizier Schubert. (Author's Collection)

had been relatively modest with ten claimed by the pilots involved. However, with more than 100 German aircraft 'mixing it' with so many Hurricanes in individual battles, it is hardly surprising that overclaiming occurred. No. 43 Sqn had soon joined No. 145 Sqn off St Catherine's Point, and an unusual confirmation of a claim came from one of the unit's groundcrew, Aircraftman De Haag. On leave on the Isle of Wight at the time, he watched his own squadron in action, confirming an aircraft claimed by Plt Off H. C. Upton had indeed crashed into the sea in flames. This was duly recorded on Upton's Combat Report for the day, opening his scoring as one of the RAF's top 'Stuka killers' of 1940–41.

That same battle on 8 August was described by Sgt Frank Carey as 'a raid so terrible and inexorable it was like trying to stop a steam roller'. His CO, Sqn Ldr J. V. C. Badger, remarked on the swarms of stepped-up aircraft. 'It was like looking up an escalator on the Piccadilly Underground'. Carey, too, made a discovery that day – it was impossible to shoot the Stuka down in its dive because the fighter simply overtook the Ju 87 as it built up speed following the aircraft. The Stuka could only be caught before it dived, or once it had pulled out.

In one of the 8 August clashes, No. 145 Sqn's Hurricanes had taken on the Ju 87s during a mid-afternoon action over the Isle of Wight. Amongst the aviators involved was Plt Off J. E. Storrar:

> As I finished my ammunition with little obvious effect, I suddenly became aware that there was a flame around his right undercarriage leg. I came up alongside. There was no sign of the rear gunner, but the pilot was looking at me and I was no more than 20 or 30 yards away. I could see his face clearly and could virtually see his hand on the stick. The flame suddenly burst over the top of the wing. Having both looked at it for what seemed like seconds, the Stuka's wing suddenly buckled – it turned over, smashed into the sea and exploded.

'Stuka killers'. Pilots of No. 501 Sqn pose for a photograph in the summer of 1940. Standing, from left to right, are Plt Off Stefan Witorzénć (two Ju 87s claimed destroyed), Flt Lt George Stoney (three Ju 87s destroyed, one probable and one damaged) and Sgt Antoni Glowacki (one Ju 87 destroyed). Seated in chairs, from left to right, are Sgt Paul Farnes (three Ju 87s destroyed) and Plt Offs Kenneth Lee (one Ju 87 damaged) and John Gibson (two Ju 87s destroyed and two damaged). Sat on the ground are Plt Offs Bob Dafforn (one Ju 87 destroyed and two damaged) and Hugh Adams, who was the only pilot in this group who did not make any Stuka claims. (Author's Collection)

I circled the smoke a couple of times and was then joined by another Hurricane from No. 145 Sqn who headed back with me towards the Sussex coast. I could see as we pulled back our hoods he was giving me the thumbs-up, and that it was Sub-Lt F. A. Smith, a pilot who had joined our squadron from the Fleet Air Arm. I then had a sudden urge to look back over my other shoulder, and saw two Messerschmitt 109s pulling behind us. I yelled "Break!" over the R/T and turned in hard towards them. As I got round to engage, I pressed the button and it just hissed – of course, no ammunition. So, I kept turning to avoid them, and they eventually disappeared. Sub-Lt Smith didn't come back and was never found. I was the last person to see him alive.

By 15 August, Stuka attacks on shipping had all but stopped, the day seeing a shift in strategy whereby the Luftwaffe focused on targeting RAF airfields (although there had already been an uncontested Stuka attack against Detling on 13 August). On the 15th, an attack on Hawkinge resulted in two Ju 87s of 10.(Stuka)/LG 1 being lost to Hurricanes of No. 501 Sqn. The next day, the airfield campaign was significantly broadened, with attacks on airfields at Tangmere, Gosport and Lee-on-Solent, as well as on the radar station at Ventnor. A total of 34 Stukas from I. and II./StG 2 were assigned Tangmere as their target, and they duly inflicted grievous damage on this important fighter airfield.

Intercepting the Stukas were Hurricanes of Nos. 43 and 601 Sqns and Spitfires of No. 602 Sqn, although the combined efforts of the fighters did not prevent or disrupt the attack. Nevertheless, nine of the raiders were brought down, with others returning damaged in a combat where it is difficult to easily establish which pilot shot down which Stuka. One of the dive-bomber losses, though, can easily be attributed through detail contained in the combat report of Flt Lt Carl Davis of No. 601 Sqn:

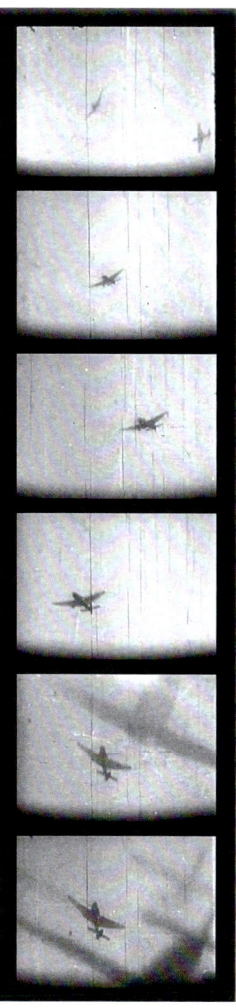

> We took off and patrolled base at 10,000ft and then were ordered to Bembridge at 20,000ft. We were then told there were bandits coming from the south and to take the top layer. Bandits were seen below coming in at about 10,000ft but could see no escort, so dived to attack. Just at this point the enemy aircraft dived for Tangmere. By the time I reached them they were at about 2,000ft, had delivered their attack, and were making for the south. I closed with one Ju 87 and after several bursts he went down under control and landed between Pagham and Bognor, crashing through some trees and a hedge. No one got out. Heavy fire, fairly accurate, and violent evasive actions were employed by the Ju 87. My aircraft was hit in the radiator, so I returned to Tangmere and landed at about 13.05 hrs.

The Stuka that he brought down ended up crashing through trees at Bowley Farm, South Mundham, mid-way between Pagham and Bognor just as Davis described. The aircraft was Wk-Nr 5618 T6+KL from 3./StG 2, its pilot, Feldwebel Heinz Rocktäschel, having been been hit and wounded. Nevertheless, he managed to bring his Stuka in for a hasty forced landing under some sort of control – albeit that it went careering through trees and a hedge. The *Bordfunker*, Oberfeldwebel Willi Witt, was already dead, his bullet-riddled body slumped in his seat. The pilot was gently lifted from the cockpit and taken to hospital in Chichester, where he died later that day.

Illustrative of the frenetic nature of RAF fighter engagements against the Stuka, this series of frames from the camera gun of Sgt Paul Farnes of No. 501 Sqn on 15 August 1940 shows his engagement with the Ju 87s of VI.(Stuka)/LG 1, after which he was credited with two of the dive-bombers destroyed. In the last two frames, a Hurricane appears between Farnes and his quarry, illustrating the danger posed by accidental friendly fire and providing a graphic example of why there was a preponderance of overclaiming in 1940 when it came to the destruction of Ju 87s. (Author's Collection)

One of the Ju 87s attacked and destroyed by No. 501 Sqn on 15 August 1940 smashed through electricity pylon wires and houses at Shorncliffe Crescent, Folkestone, resulting in the death of both crewmen. In the distance, five Hurricanes can be seen heading east, these possibly being the aircraft of No. 501 Sqn returning to Hawkinge. (Author's Collection)

In the same action, American Plt Off 'Billy' Fiske, also from No. 601 Sqn, landed his burning Hurricane at Tangmere. Although rescued from his aircraft, he too died in hospital the following day. It remains unclear as to how Fiske's Hurricane was set on fire, although it must have happened during the clash with the Stuka formation. It had been a bloody day of battles for the dive-bomber force, and engagements two days later would see even greater ferocity.

Recognised as the hardest-fought day of the battle, the story of 18 August 1940 has been recounted in various publications but suffice to say that it would see the end of major Stuka operations against land-based targets in Britain. It would also see heavy losses for the dive-bomber force, and as an account of what it was like to be on the receiving end of fighter attacks in the Stuka, none come more visceral than that by 2./StG 77 pilot Feldwebel Günther Meyer-Bothling, who took part in the raid against Thorney Island that day:

Shortly before the target, the formation was attacked by fighters. My *Bordfunker*, Unteroffizier Erhardt Schulz, warned me of many Hurricanes attacking from the starboard rear. As the attack was from the right-hand side, I tried to out-turn the Hurricanes as Schulz opened fire. Then he reported a further attack by Spitfires, and at the same time he told me we had already taken hits. I can still hear Schulz's words – "Ah, you shit! Spitfire from port!" This was followed by impacts and a scream from Schulz. He was killed instantly. Bullets shot past me, right and left, thanks to the armour plate, but shattered most of the instruments in the panel, including the compass. One bullet creased my head, another cut my waist, which also tore my parachute harness. To bail out would now be futile, as I would have fallen out of the harness. All I could do was stand the Stuka on its nose and try to get away in a vertical dive.

During the dive, I tried to jettison the bombs, but the system didn't work. I pulled the manual release and got rid of the main bomb and the two from the left wing, before pulling out and heading for home. Next, I tore off my flying helmet because blood was pouring down my neck and took off my neckerchief and held it to my wound with my right hand.

Still over England, I came under fire from the ground and had to pull the stick suddenly and jink to port, and hold the machine horizontal, although the trimming no longer worked. Then I decided to jettison the hood to get some fresh air but was hit in the face by a disgusting mist of oil, and when I glanced down, I saw that the window in the floor was also coated in oil. So, an oil pipe or the tank had been hit. But what now? It was frightening.

The engine was still running, but for how much longer? I considered a forced landing in England, but the fields were small and ground fire hit me in the right wing. I was grasped with cold rage; it didn't matter what happened, I must keep flying!

I finally reached the sea, saw parachutes in the sky, a Junkers 87 down in the sea and then, suddenly, another Junkers 87 alongside me! It was Unteroffizier Nagel, and I made him understand by hand signals to stay with me. He guided me to the French coast because I had no compass. And then it happened – I was directly over the beach north of Bayeux when the propeller stopped. I had only one option: to get down on the beach. Luckily, although the legs dug in, I didn't turn over. I was back, although Erhardt's body was hanging lifelessly from his straps in the rear cockpit.

Although the Battle of Britain was far from over, all VIII. *Fliegerkorps* Ju 87 units in the Cotentin Peninsula were transferred to II. *Fliegerkorps* in the Pas-de-Calais on 19 August following a temporary suspension of Stuka operations against the British Isles. There were sound operational reasons for that transfer, although they were not connected to the supposed 'unacceptable losses' of Stukas as is often presented. The Air Ministry, in its 1948 narrative on the battle, accurately summed up the reasons:

After 18 August they [Ju 87s] were withdrawn from the battle, the intention being to use them against Channel shipping when an invasion expedition was launched. This accounts for the concentration of dive-bombers in the Pas-de-Calais during the first days of September, and their complete inactivity during that and the following months.

This move was a new disposal of forces in preparation for the invasion itself. The dive-bombers were now placed in a tactical position for army support in the coming invasion in a similar manner to the other continental campaigns.

Meanwhile, the day and night Blitz evolved into a night Blitz only, the bomber force protected from interception by the cover of darkness. On a strategic front, the German military decided that a wider solution for dealing with Britain lay in starving

Soldiers remove belted 7.92mm ammunition from the battered wreck of the Ju 87B of 3./StG 2 that was shot down on 16 August by Flt Lt C. R. Davis in a Hurricane of No. 601 Sqn. The aircraft crashed through trees at Bowley Farm, South Mundham, shortly after attacking RAF Tangmere. Both crewmen died, the *Bordfunker* being killed in the air and the pilot subsequently succumbing to his wounds in hospital. (Author's Collection)

During the early afternoon of
18 August 1940, a large force of
Ju 87s from I./StG 77 targeting
RAF Thorney Island were
intercepted by Hurricanes of
Nos. 43 and 601 Sqns and
Spitfires of No. 602 Sqn. To the
east of the target, over
Fishbourne in West Sussex, Plt
Off C. K. Gray, flying as 'Yellow 3'
in a Hurricane I of No. 43 Sqn, was
forced to break off a successful
attack when his windscreen was
coated in oil from the Stuka he
was shooting at. Ju 87B Wk-Nr
5518 of 2./StG 77 was being
flown by Oberleutnant Johannes
Wilhelm, who was also coated in
oil as he exited the cockpit of the
dive-bomber and took to his
parachute. His *Bordfunker*,
Unteroffizier Anton Wörner, also
escaped by parachute and broke
both of his legs upon landing.
Meanwhile, the Stuka dived into
Fishbourne Channel, Chichester
Harbour, taking its bomb load
with it. The details contained in
Plt Off Gray's combat report
confirm beyond doubt that
Wilhelm's aircraft was the Stuka
with which he was credited.

its population of food supplies through air and sea attacks on shipping, and Generalfeldmarschall Hermann Göring, Commander-in-Chief of the Luftwaffe, issued a further directive:

Attacks, [to be carried out] with fighter escort, on convoys in the Channel and on assemblies of shipping in the Thames.

The Stukas were back in business.

Executing the order, III./StG 1 was detailed for an attack on vessels in the Thames Estuary at 1430 hrs on 1 November. With around 20 Stukas, Oberleutnant Helmut Mahlke led an action that he described as inconclusive, although his dive-bombers did sink the coaster SS *Letchworth* and the Oaze Light Vessel – officially, Trinity House Light Vessel (LV) 60. Certainly, the light vessel performed an important function as the assembly point for south coast convoys, controlling safe passage at an entrance to a defensively mined area. Unfortunately, its six crew were lost when LV 60 was sent to the bottom. Joining it was the minesweeper HMT *Tilbury Ness,* a victim of the same attack.

During the raid, 5./StG 1 lost Stuka Wk-Nr 5227 6G+KS flown by Gefreiter Werner Karach and *Bordfunker* Gefreiter Max Aulehner. Karach was presumed dead, whilst Aulehner was thrown clear and rescued, unhurt. Almost certainly, Karach's aircraft had been lost to the Spitfire of either Plt Off M. C. Kinder or Plt Off C. H. Saunders, both from No. 92 Sqn, with Kinder claiming a Ju 87 destroyed and another probably destroyed and Saunders claiming one destroyed.

Throughout November 1940 Stuka shipping attacks continued, with the last massed operation taking place on the 14th. Once more, Mahlke would lead:

The last mission of this era was a fiasco from the very start, and although our escort fighters met us and flew with us across the English Channel, things soon started to go wrong. We had been sent out to attack shipping that had been reported in the Dover Straits area – a convoy, in fact. When we got there, there were no ships to be seen. Although that was annoying, we did have a secondary target – the Dover radar station. So, as we flew down towards Dover, and as we had seen no ships, we had to prepare for an attack on the big pylons. Then, getting close to Dover, our fighter escort left us because the pilots did not want to get caught in the Dover flak barrage, and they stood off some distance from us. This wasn't helpful, and we were soon in a disastrously exposed and dangerous position.

Emerging from the haze, Mahlke could see approaching specks growing larger as they raced towards his formation of 40 Stukas – RAF fighters. Meanwhile, the protective escorts exited 'stage-left' and loitered in the distance, out of reach of anti-aircraft guns but unable to come to the aid of the Stukas or provide essential close-cover protection. Furthermore, if the distant escorts had not seen the incoming fighters, then nothing could be done to alert them because they were on a different radio frequency to the Ju 87s.

The aircraft closing on III./StG 1 were Spitfires of Nos. 66 and 74 Sqns, and although the escorts did eventually engage the RAF fighters, it was too late to avoid

One of the most famous Stuka photographs of the Battle of Britain captures the final seconds of a stricken aircraft from 3./StG 77 plummeting to its destruction over the rooftops of Chichester after being engaged by Hurricanes of No. 43 Sqn on 18 August 1940. Its crew, Unteroffizier August Dann and Unteroffizier Erich Kohl, were both killed. (Author's Collection)

the mayhem they duly wreaked upon the dive-bombers. At once, the Stuka pilots were more intent on avoiding attack or collision, despite the masts of the radar station being in sight. There was no chance of setting the formation up in the correct position for an attack. Nevertheless, some of the Stukas did manage to target the Port of Dover, causing damage to harbour installations.

In the confusion, many Spitfire pilots shot at and claimed the same Stuka destroyed. Although two *did* eventually go down, there were multiple claims in a classic case of over-scoring. In this single battle, No. 66 Sqn claimed two destroyed, with three unconfirmed and three damaged, whilst No. 74 Sqn claimed 14 destroyed, two unconfirmed and three damaged. There was no doubting the engagement's ferocity, as Mahlke recalled:

Surprisingly, at the end of 1940, the Ju 87 was employed on a few night operations against London and Dover, and on occasional nocturnal anti-shipping sorties in the Thames Estuary area, being protected from RAF fighter interference by the cover of darkness. (Author's Collection)

> All the aircraft from my unit bar one went home with hits that day. I think the most hits we counted on one aircraft was 82. The pilot who got home unscathed was one of my *Staffelkapitäne*, Oberleutnant Schairer. He got away because he successfully outmanoeuvred many attacks by the Spitfires.

Singly, or in straggling groups, Mahlke's battered Stukas fled back across the Channel, low on the water, as fast as they could go:

> This event was good evidence of the quality of the Ju 87, as well as the poor quality of senior leadership. The officer who commanded the mission knew much about fighter tactics, but very little about Stukas. It was the first time such an operation had been ordered and planned by a fighter leader, but it was a complete failure.

One of the two Ju 87s sent crashing into the Channel was the 9. *Staffel* machine flown by Oberleutnant Otto Blumers and his *Bordfunker*, Gefreiter Willy Koch. Fished out of the Channel, Blumers was taken prisoner and interrogated. RAF intelligence subsequently reported:

> In the afternoon six aircraft from his *Staffel* took off and flew north-westwards to join about fourteen other Ju 87s and a strong fighter escort. They flew across the Channel to the North Foreland, and then along the coast to Dover at a height of about 10,000ft.
>
> When approaching Dover, and before having made any attack, the formation was intercepted by about twenty Spitfires who were flying straight towards them. The Spitfires did not attack immediately, but circled round and delivered attacks from the rear. The second burst of machine gun fire set his aircraft on fire and he bailed out and landed in the water, being picked up by an MTB [motor torpedo boat] and taken into Dover. The wireless operator, whom he left to his fate, is presumed to have been killed in the crash.

It was the end of massed Stuka operations against the British Isles, an end hastened by deteriorating weather, shortening daylight hours and lack of targets. Surprisingly though, several night attacks on London were made by Stukas during the winter of 1940–41.

On 5 February 1941, Stuka operations against Britain had their last gasp as an unescorted sortie by a *Kette* of three aircraft of 2./StG 1 was engaged by four Spitfires of No. 92 Sqn patrolling from Manston. Plt Offs R. H. Fokes and C. H. Saunders and Sgts H. Bowen-Morris and C. A. Ream had taken off at 0845 hrs and were near Ramsgate an hour later when Red 2 (Saunders) spotted an explosion below, the pilots first thinking a ship had struck a mine because they saw no aircraft. As they went down to look, they met a lone Ju 87 approaching them at 5,000ft.

Fokes attacked head-on, as did Saunders, but the Stuka twisted and turned as it tried to get away, the pursuit literally turning into a dogfight as each Spitfire chased the dive-bomber, jockeying to get into firing position as the aircraft snaked around the sky. Eventually, the four pilots drove the Stuka over land and Fokes got a beam shot into the aircraft as it turned, causing the dive-bomber to blow up and crash. Coincidentally, this was right over Manston, where the squadron's CO, Sqn Ldr 'Johnny' Kent, was on hand to witness a victory shared by four of his pilots:

Having been on the first patrol of the morning, I had been back to the Mess for breakfast and was just returning to Dispersal when I heard gunfire. I stopped the car and got out to stare in amazement at the sight of one lone Stuka weaving madly to avoid the attention of four Spitfires. All five were coming towards me, and it occurred to me that I was in the line of fire, so I hid behind a vehicle that was handy. Then I saw a notice on it reading 100 Octane – it was one of the refuelling bowsers. So, I darted back to my car! Just as I reached it, the Stuka reached the edge of the airfield almost directly above me at about a hundred feet. Here he was headed off by one of the Spitfires, and I could clearly see both gunner and pilot in their cockpits with the De Wilde ammunition bursting around them. The Spitfire overshot and pulled away, and the German made another desperate attempt to land and turned violently to port, but at this instant Plt Off Fokes, in my aeroplane, flashed past me and gave a short burst with the cannons. I can still hear the 'thump-thump-thump' of them followed by the terrific 'whoosh' as the Stuka blew up and crashed just outside the boundary of the airfield.

The aircraft was Wk-Nr 5225 J9+BK, flown by Leutnant Ernst Schimmelpfennig with *Bordfunker* Obergefreiter Hans Kaden. Both men were killed when the Stuka exploded upon hitting the ground. The other Stukas escaped unseen by the four pilots, who had focused on their single quarry and did not spot the other raiders in poor visibility.

Describing the engagement between the 2./StG 1 Stuka and the four Spitfires of No. 92 Sqn as a 'dogfight' might well be regarded as far-fetched. However, we turn again to Helmut Mahlke to put this encounter into perspective:

Experience in air combat had shown in many cases that the Ju 87 could outmanoeuvre up to five simultaneously attacking Spitfires if the pilot had enough experience to observe all attackers sufficiently and to take necessary defensive measures at the right moment. As a rule, these were low speed and counter-curves to attack with fixed machine guns against the approaching fighter, and although with two fixed guns no great successes

Spitfire IB R6923/QJ-S of No. 92 Sqn was one of the four fighters from this unit that engaged and shot down a Ju 87 of 2./StG 1 over RAF Manston on 5 February 1941. On that occasion, the Spitfire was being flown by Plt Off R. H. Fokes. (Author's Collection)

The four victorious pilots of No. 92 Sqn inspect their handiwork at RAF Manston on 5 February 1941 – Plt Off R. H. Fokes is standing closest to the fuselage. The aircraft was Wk-Nr 5225 J9+BK, flown by Leutnant Ernst Schimmelpfennig and *Bordfunker* Obergefreiter Hans Kaden, who were both killed. (Author's Collection)

could be expected, the massive-looking Ju 87, when flying stubbornly on collision course towards the fighter, always had such an impressive effect that the fighter preferred to turn away before it could fire a properly aimed burst.

The most difficult thing was to outmanoeuvre several fighters when they attacked from different directions at the same time. They all had to be watched simultaneously to catch the moment when one of them would have to open fire if he wanted to hit something. At that moment, a quick yank on the stick was enough to make the aircraft jump up so that the fighter's salvo passed under the Ju 87.

Since an escape was out of the question due to the low speed of the Ju 87 in relation to the fighter, the Ju 87 had to 'oppose' until the fighters had expanded their ammunition. In this respect, it should be mentioned that in many cases after such a dogfight – when the ammunition had been exhausted – the British fighters flew close to the Ju 87 in parallel flight and signed off with a sporting military salute before heading home in a half-roll. After these air battles, the Ju 87s were usually brought home damaged to a greater or lesser extent, but they were robust enough to give the experienced pilot the absolute feeling of safety in air combat. In one case, a Ju 87 belonging to a *Staffelkapitän* returned from a mission without a single hit, after a whole squadron of Spitfires had fired off all their ammunition in the dogfight with the Stuka.

In their engagements with the Stuka during 1940–41, the RAF's fighter pilots gave a good account of themselves. But so had the Stuka crews. And many an RAF fighter pilot was stymied and frustrated in his efforts to bring the aircraft down. Not always had the Ju 87 been 'easy meat'.

STATISTICS AND ANALYSIS

Luftwaffe air activity had increased to a peak after the launch of the *Blitzkrieg* on 10 May 1940 and up to the Dunkirk evacuations in early June. Thereafter, the air assault against Britain gathered further pace, leading to the commencement of the Battle of Britain on 10 July 1940. However, it was in France that Hurricanes first engaged the Stuka, where the Luftwaffe had 360 in its Order of Battle.

In a pattern repeated in the use of the Stuka against Britain, however, overclaiming by RAF pilots in France was rife. From 10 May until the fall of France on 22 June, a total of 110 Stukas were 'confirmed' as victories, with a further 37 claimed as probables. Thus, potentially 147 Stukas fell to the guns of Hurricanes in little more than a month. Against this high figure it is necessary to consider those other Ju 87s during the period that were lost to anti-aircraft fire, accidents and the many claimed by fighter pilots of other Allied air forces. If that is set against the *actual* total of Stukas lost up until the fall of France, then the true scale of RAF overclaiming can be seen – the total number of Stukas lost to *all* causes during the period in question was 120.

Whilst this figure is significant out of a force of 360 (i.e. exactly one-third), it is important to note that these losses were rapidly made good in terms of equipment and personnel. By the end of the campaign, all units were back to almost full strength.

No. 43 Sqn enjoyed greater success against the Ju 87 than any other unit during the Battle of Britain. Here, pilots from the squadron admire a trophy taken from one of the 16 August 1940 Tangmere raiders in the form of the *Staffel* emblem of 3./StG 2 hacked from the wreckage of a Stuka they had downed that day. (Author's Collection)

Although the Stuka force had indeed taken a heavy hit, it was the case, thus far, that the German war machine was able to make good the losses of men and materiel. However, it was not a situation which could go on *ad infinitum,* and it would clearly have become necessary to better husband the Stuka force if the war in France had dragged on. However, figures taken from the Luftwaffe Quartermaster General's returns of 10 August 1940 show that 327 Ju 87s were ready and available for combat operations against Britain.

In terms of RAF fighter claims, over France and later, it was invariably the case that where groups of fighters engaged groups of Stukas then claims were correspondingly high. This can be attributed to the fact that multiple pilots clamoured for position to attack the same target. Then, when that target was hit, several pilots would claim the same aircraft, each believing they were the victor. The similarity between combats, and the sheer confusion of such engagements, led to intelligence officers being unable to properly unravel events and accurately apportion victories. In this way, overclaiming against the Stuka force became the very nature of the beast.

If RAF fighter pilots became preoccupied with engaging the Stukas – which sometimes happened – then woe betide them if they were pounced upon by any escorting fighters. Many a pilot was shot down while engaging Stuka formations. This was a particular danger during such interceptions, and the fictional scene in the 1969 film *Battle of Britain* when RAF pilots are engaging Stukas comes to mind. In that scene, one pilot excitedly exclaims 'It's easier than shooting rats in a barrel', to which his CO snaps 'You'll be in a barrel if you don't look out for the fighters!' That said, the Stuka was not entirely helpless when it came to defending itself.

Although the pair of forward-firing 7.92mm MG 17 machine guns were largely for self-defence in the event of frontal attack, they could also be used for ground strafing or for ranging purposes when gauging the bomb release point when targeting ships. To the rear, one flexibly mounted 7.92mm MG 15 machine gun, operated by the *Bordfunker,* provided a meagre defence to any attack from behind. When flown in cohesive formations, however, the combined firepower of the group of aircraft could be considerable. When trained on a chasing fighter, which would frequently close to just a matter of yards, a single MG 15 could be a dauntingly lethal weapon. And there

Ju 87B-1 Wk-Nr 5167 S2+UN of 5./StG 77 force-landed on Ham Manor golf course at Angmering, near Littlehampton, after the attack on Ford (HMS *Peregrine*) airfield on 18 August 1940. Both crewmen were seriously wounded by fire from the Spitfire I of No. 602 Sqn's Sgt B. E. P. Whall, who subsequently claimed a second dive-bomber from III./StG 77 also destroyed. During the course of the second engagement, Whall's fighter was hit by return fire from the *Bordfunker,* forcing him to ditch into the shallows off Elmer Sands at Middleton-on-Sea. (Author's Collection)

ENGAGING THE ENEMY

The Spitfire I/IB/II, Hurricane I and Gladiator II were all equipped with a Barr & Stroud GM 2 reflector gunsight. Depicted here is the sight mounted in a Hurricane I, which is engaging a formation of Ju 87's. The gunsight, created by the company in 1936, featured a lens through which a large circular graticule was projected onto an angled circular glass reflector screen 76mm in diameter. The graticule was bisected by a cross, the horizontal bar of which was broken in the centre. The range/base settings could be set via two knurled rings. The internal mechanism then set the sight according to range. The radius of the graticule ring helped the pilot gauge deflection allowances for an aircraft crossing the ring of the sight. The gunsight was illuminated by a half-silvered 12-volt lamp and the sight itself was mounted onto a cross member above the instrument panel. It had a substantial rubber crash pad to prevent injury to the pilot in the event of a crash. In service during 1940–41, the GM 2 was known as the Reflector Sight Mark II.

Ju 87B-2 REAR COCKPIT

The rear cockpit position of the Stuka in use during 1940–41 varied in numerous respects between the Ju 87B-1 and B-2 variants, with the rear cockpit of the Ju 87R following the pattern of the B-2 (illustrated here). Officially, the position was occupied by the *Bordfunker*, who also operated a single rearward-firing MG 15 machine gun mounted in a fully rotatable ball-and-socket arrangement which, in turn, was installed inside a fully rotatable gun ring as part of the rearmost cockpit canopy. There were racks for full (75 rounds) 7.92mm ammunition drums and a stowage box for them once they were empty. The *Bordfunker* sat on a revolving seat which could be swivelled to face forward and allow him to operate the FuG radio set. The whole rear section of the canopy was jettisonable should the *Bordfunker* need to escape. The position was protected by eight-millimetre steel armour plating beneath the gun mounting and extending beneath the floor of the *Bordfunker's* position.

are certainly cases of Stuka crews being officially credited with victories through the destruction of fighters.

The first two such instances which appear to have been recorded occurred during the Battle of France. Both saw claims against French fighters. The first was a Morane-Saulnier MS.406 shot down six miles southeast of Saint-Omer at 2025 hrs on 22 May 1940 by Feldwebel Salendin of 9./StG 2. The second victory came on 13 June when Unteroffizier Werner Brehm of *Stab* I./StG 77 shot down a Curtiss Hawk 75A-1 over Labelot at 1250 hrs. In both instances, it is presumed that the claimant was probably the *Bordfunker*.

While RAF fighters may have been claimed by Stukas over France, none have been found in Luftwaffe archives. It was not until Ju 87 operations took place over Britain in the summer that further claims are recorded. The first is logged as taking place at 1352 hrs (Central European Time) on 16 August over Selsey Bill when Obergefreiter Hermann Witznick of 9./StG 2 claimed a Hurricane destroyed. Also on that day, Unteroffizier Ludwig Bosch of 8./StG 2 was credited with the destruction of a Spitfire over the English coast, while Hauptmann Heinrich Brücker of *Stab III.*/StG 2 claimed a Hurricane over the Channel. It is likely that Witznick and Bosch were flying as *Bordfunker* in their respective aircraft, but Brücker would have been the pilot. In the latter case, a fighter probably presented itself in front of Brücker's guns after it overtook the Stuka, at which point he attacked it. As to the claim by Witznick, the possibility cannot be excluded that he was responsible for hitting Hurricane P3358 of No. 601 Sqn flown by Plt Off 'Billy' Fiske, who landed his burning aircraft at Tangmere during the attack on the airfield.

During the air assaults of 18 August, the Stuka force again made another claim over an RAF fighter. This time, Oberleutnant Bronk of 2./StG 77 was credited with downing a Spitfire over RAF Thorney Island at 1520 hrs (Central European Time). It was, though, meagre retribution for the losses sustained during an attack which cost StG 77 alone a total of 14 aircraft shot down (some 20 per cent of the force it committed), ten damaged, 25 crew members killed, seven wounded and six captured. Overall, during that operation, the *Stukawaffe* lost 13 per cent of its total force. Nevertheless, despite grievous losses, StG 77 alone had returned to full strength in both men and aircraft inside a week.

Of the Ju 87 casualties on 18 August, it is often claimed this resulted in withdrawal of the type because of unacceptable losses. There is no evidence that this was the case. And if losses had been so catastrophically unacceptable, then one might have expected at least some units to have been stood down or subsumed into others. None were.

1. Rotatable gun ring
2. Flexible ball-and-socket Ikaria Z10d gun mount
3. MG 15 7.92mm machine gun
4. Spare MG 15 75-round magazines in racks
5. Empty magazine stowage container
6. Rotatable seat base
7. MG 15 tools and spares kit

8. Service gas mask in container
9. Seat lap strap
10. Rotatable seat pan frame, recessed for parachute pack
11. Seat position lock
12. Rear canopy position lock
13. Sliding/jettisonable rear cockpit cover
14. Empty 7.92mm cartridge case container

A similar view was shared during a 1983 conference at the US Army War College attended by Major Paul-Werner Hozzel, formerly of I./StG 1. At the event, Professor John Stolfi put forward a view that while Stuka losses over Britain in 1940 were severe, it was necessary to look at it statistically and 'spread the thing out in time'. In other words, one should look at Stuka losses in the context of other German bomber types – for example, the He 111. Stolfi suggested that whilst there were no single attacks during which the He 111 suffered comparable grievous losses, they ultimately endured just as high a rate of attrition, if not higher, throughout the battle. The same could be said of other German bomber types.

Perhaps, too, a statement by Air Chief Marshal Sir Hugh Dowding, Commander-in-Chief of RAF Fighter Command in 1940, in his 1941 despatch on the Battle of Britain added to a false narrative concerning the Ju 87. In it, he stated that the Stuka was 'nothing short of a death-trap, and formations of Ju 87s were practically annihilated on several occasions'. Near annihilation was never the case, although formations did suffer badly, as we have seen. Even on 18 August it was a very long way from an 'annihilation'. But perhaps Dowding's perception of annihilation was based on the high victory claims by his pilots for Ju 87s destroyed that came across his desk?

While some RAF pilots certainly made over-optimistic claims to bolster personal scores, the majority of 'overclaimed' victories were the result of a genuine belief that the aircraft claimed as destroyed actually *had* been destroyed. In the case of engagements with Stukas, as we have seen, confusion often reigned. Individual pilots frequently got in the way of each other as they engaged, resulting in multiple pilots claiming the same Ju 87 as destroyed, while oblivious to the fact that others had claimed the same aircraft.

With the entirety of the Stuka force relocated to the Pas-de-Calais region from 19 August, none fell to RAF fighters during this period of stand-down. Attrition through accidents continued, however, with 19 Stukas written off and several crew members killed or injured.

On 1 November, and through to early 1941, a resumption of Stuka activity against British targets resulted in a further nine dive-bombers being lost to RAF guns. Once again, overclaiming saw RAF fighter pilots claim 37 Stukas destroyed and 15 probably destroyed. It is worth noting, too, that if the Stuka's withdrawal from operations over Britain in August had been anything at all to do with unacceptable losses, then why was the aircraft brought back into action over Britain from November 1940 through to early 1941? After all, nothing had changed. If anything, the RAF's fighter force was stronger than ever, and it was certainly more practised in countering the Stuka than it had been during the high summer of 1940.

By the end of December 1940, total RAF fighter claims for Stukas destroyed stood at 171 confirmed, 63 probably destroyed, and 56 damaged. Again, this represented overclaiming by a huge margin. The true number of Stuka losses (to *all* causes, including accidents) during this period was 101 destroyed and 84 damaged.

During the Thorney Island raid on 18 August 1940, *Bordfunker* Unteroffizier Karl Maier of 1./StG 77 was hit eight times in the body by bullets fired by RAF fighters and injured by flying metal and Perspex splinters. Miraculously, he somehow escaped serious injury. (Author's Collection)

Ranged against the Luftwaffe at the commencement of the Battle of Britain, the RAF had 644 frontline fighters. During the course of the campaign, it lost no fewer than 1,049 fighters, with 535 pilots killed or missing and ten captured. Of these losses, it is difficult to ascertain exactly how many were *directly* attributable to operations against the Stuka force because a large number of them (aside from those claims made by Ju 87 crews) were the result of engagements by fighters that were either peripheral to or not directly related to the dive-bomber operations *per se*.

However, just as they had been for the Stuka force, the RAF's aircraft losses were always made good. And although the strength of RAF Fighter Command in terms of available fighters stood at 644 at the start of the Battle of Britain in July, it had risen to 708 on 1 August, 746 on 1 September and 734 on 1 October.

For the RAF, the end of the Battle of Britain might perhaps be seen as a 'home draw', their opponents not quite being able to push victory over the line. And whatever the rate of attrition, the Stuka force always managed to make good its losses, being able to do so right up until it left the theatre of operations in early 1941.

As a sergeant pilot with Nos. 3 and 43 Sqns, Frank Carey destroyed five Ju 87s and claimed a further three as probably destroyed between 13 May and 18 August 1940. Photographed here as a group captain in late 1944 while serving as CO of No. 73 OTU at Abu Sueir, in Egypt, Carey survived the war with a total of 25 and three shared victories, four unconfirmed destroyed, three probable, one 'possible' and eight damaged to his name. (Author's Collection)

LEADING 'STUKA KILLERS' IN 1940–41

At least 154 RAF fighter pilots were credited with one or more Ju 87s destroyed during the period between 10 May 1940 and 5 February 1941. Of these individuals, 17 pilots were credited with three Stukas destroyed. The highest scoring pilots were:

- Sgt Herbert Hallowes of No. 43 Sqn – six Stukas (final score, all types, 17 and 2 shared destroyed)

- Plt Off Hamilton Charles Upton of No. 43 Sqn – six Stukas (final score, all types, ten and one shared destroyed)

- Plt Off Frank Reginald Carey of Nos. 3 and 43 Sqns – five Stukas (final score, all types, 25 and three shared destroyed)

- Flt Lt Nicholas Gresham Cooke of No. 264 Sqn – five Stukas (final score, all types, nine and three shared)

Flt Lt Nicholas Cooke was paired with his air gunner, Cpl Albert Lippett, during all his operations in 1940. The pair were shot down and killed in Defiant L6975 over the Dunkirk area on 31 May 1940 during an attack on He 111s of KG 27. For the operation on 29 May, when the pair were credited with five Stukas destroyed in a single engagement, Cooke was awarded an immediate DFC and Lippett an immediate DFM.

INDEX